The Quest for Unity in the New Testament Church

The Quest for Unity in the New Testament Church

A Study in Paul and Acts

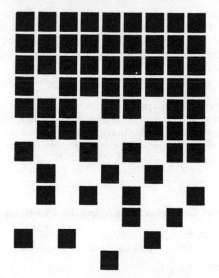

Paul J. Achtemeier

FORTRESS PRESS   PHILADELPHIA

Library of Congress Cataloging-in-Publication Data

Achtemeier, Paul J.
  The quest for unity in the New Testament church.

  Bibliography: p.
  Includes index.
  1. Church—Unity—Biblical teaching. 2. Bible.
N.T. Epistles of Paul —Criticism, interpretation, etc.
3. Bible. N.T. Acts—Criticism, interpretation, etc.
I. Title.
BS2545.C5A25 1987   270.1   86-45911
ISBN 0-8006-1972-2

2669186   Printed in the United States of America   1-1972

To
Raymond E. Brown, S.S.
Joseph A. Fitzmyer, S.J.
James L. Mays
Scholars, Churchmen, Friends
This book is dedicated
as an expression
of gratitude

CONTENTS

PREFACE

The immediate impetus for the research that has resulted in the publication of this book derived from my need to prepare the presidential address to be delivered to the Catholic Biblical Association at its forty-eighth General Meeting at the University of San Francisco, in August 1985. That preliminary account of some of the evidence and conclusions appeared as "An Elusive Unity: Paul, Acts, and the Early Church" in the *Catholic Biblical Quarterly* (vol. 48, 1986, pp. 1–26). From a broader perspective, however, the topic is one that has engaged my attention for some time, and I am grateful to the CBA for giving me the opportunity I needed to get the research underway. The impetus for continuing the research and expanding its broader results into book form derive from the interest of John A. Hollar of Fortress Press, who urged me to prepare a book-length treatment of this subject. It is due to those two causes that I have pursued a more detailed study relating to some New Testament aspects of my general interest in the problem of early church unity, and have written the pages that follow.

Even so modest an undertaking as this is possible only with the help of many people; it is now my pleasant duty to acknowledge that help. Much of the material was broached, defended, refined, and discussed with my wife, without whose keen insights little I have done would have had such quality as it may have possessed. Without the help of Martha Aycock, research librarian at Union Theological Seminary, the task would have been far more difficult than it was; her cheerful disposition and ability to provide any resource, however obscure, contributes to the joy of scholarship. Two institutions deserve my thanks: the Catholic Biblical Association of America for the honor it granted me in electing me its president for 1985, and Union Theological Seminary in Virginia for granting me a sabbatical leave (eight months) and a partial leave of absence (four months) during which much of this work was done.

This book is dedicated to three scholars whose colleagueship has been precious to me, and whom in calling friends I honor myself. While they of course have no responsibility for the content of this book, each in his own way has contributed to my appreciation of sound scholarship and true piety, and I wish at this time publicly to acknowledge that debt. One of the chief joys of my academic career has been the privilege of associating with such colleagues as these.

PAUL J. ACHTEMEIER
Union Theological Seminary
Richmond, Va.
Ascension Day, 1986

ABBREVIATIONS

AB	Anchor Bible
An Bib	Analecta biblica
Aus BR	*Australian Biblical Review*
BJRL	*Bulletin of the John Rylands University Library of Manchester*
B Sac	*Bibliotheca Sacra*
BZ	*Biblische Zeitschrift*
CM	*Christian Ministry*
CTM	*Concordia Theological Monthly*
Cur TM	*Currents in Theology and Mission*
CV	*Communio Viatorum*
EKK	Evangelische-Katholischer Kommentar zum Neuen Testament
Exp Tim	*Expository Times*
HNT	Handbuch zum Neuen Testament
HTKNT	Herders theologischer Kommentar zum Neuen Testament
HTR	*Harvard Theological Review*
ITQ	*Irish Theological Quarterly*
JAAR	*Journal of the American Academy of Religion*
JBC	R. E. Brown et al., eds. *The Jerome Biblical Commentary.* Englewood Cliffs, N.J.: Prentice-Hall, 1968.
JBL	*Journal of Biblical Literature*
JBR	*Journal of Bible and Religion*
JEvTS	*Journal of the Evangelical Theological Society*
JQR	*Jewish Quarterly Review*
JSNT	*Journal for the Study of the New Testament*

KEK   Kritisch-Exegetischer Kommentar
LCL   Loeb Classical Library
Meyer K   H. A. W. Meyer, Kritisch-exegetischer Kommentar über
          das Neuen Testament
NovT   *Novum Testamentum*
NTS   *New Testament Studies*
RB   *Revue biblique*
RSR   *Recherches de science religieuse*
SBL DS   Society of Biblical Literature Dissertation Series
ST   *Studia Theologica*
St. VTQ   *St. Vladimir's Theological Quarterly*
THKNT   Theologischer Handkommentar zum Neuen Testament
TLZ   *Theologische Literaturzeitung*
WUNT   Wissenschaftliche Untersuchungen zum Neuen Testament
ZKT   *Zeitschrift für katholische Theologie*
ZNW   *Zeitschrift für die neutestamentliche Wissenschaft*
ZTK   *Zeitschrift für Theologie und Kirche*

INTRODUCTION

The problem concerning the nature and extent of the unity that existed within the early church is an issue that is as theologically important as it is historically complex. The theological importance hardly needs comment, given the ecumenical activity and discussion, across not only denominational but also religious lines, that has occurred during the past few decades. That the historical problems involved are of daunting complexity needs no further demonstration than the kind of books that have been written by those who have sought to trace the relations among the various Christian communities during the first years of those communities' existence.

The impression which is held by many, scholars and nonscholars alike, of an initial unity gradually threatened by increasing heresy is due almost exclusively to the picture one gains from a reading of the Book of Acts in the New Testament.[1] That such a picture of unity in Acts owes at least as much to Luke's hindsight as it does to any form of historical reality has long been known by those who have attempted to give the narrative in Acts more than a quick reading; any scholarly commentary on Acts will make that evident at once. Add to that the evidence about problems with such unity contained in the other New Testament writings (e.g., the letters of Paul, especially Galatians, the Gospels of Matthew and Mark, the Letters of John[2]), and it is evident that not even within the New Testament is there convincing evidence of a simple, early unity within the church.

Yet because of the importance of the theological issues involved, one is forced, despite the complex and often tenuous nature of the historical evidence, to identify as closely as possible the situation within which the early church found itself vis-à-vis its unity, and the threats

1

to that unity which it faced. The major theological issue, simply put, is this: Unless we are aware of the problems the early church faced concerning its unity, we will inevitably romanticize that period and either give up in despair at the course taken by subsequent developments in the history of the church, or else assume in a naive way that all it takes to recover that lost, original unity is a little good will and some pleasant negotiations.

Neither alternative is valid, as I hope to show in this book. Unless we are clearly aware that such a romantic view of an original unity does not stand up under historical scrutiny, all contemporary attempts to achieve unity will be unrealistic about the problems facing that quest. The evidence in the New Testament is clear: The church, from its beginning, faced problems of division and disunity, with the result that such unity still remains a goal to be achieved in the life of the visible body of Christ. Only a clear, hard-eyed view of the kind of problems that have beset the Christian community from its beginning will enable that community to move forward, under the guidance of God's Spirit, to that unity to which it is called.

Within the scope of this book, we cannot, of course, cover all the threats to unity, and the kinds of and reasons for division within the New Testament churches. Nor is it our intention to show how, given a hard look at the state of the earliest church, the ecumenical movement in the present generation ought to proceed. What we shall try to do, however, is analyze the evidence concerning one key problem in the early church: the relationship between Jewish and gentile Christians. We will analyze that problem from an even more specific perspective, namely, how that problem revealed itself in the relationship between the apostle Paul and the religious authorities in the Jewish Christian community in Jerusalem. We shall attempt to see if we can recover a realistic picture of the conflict into which the earliest Christian community was thrust by reason of its very nature as a movement that was born from within the religion of Judaism, and that understood itself to possess a worldwide mission.

Finally, let it be noted at the outset that the key point in the following discussion of Paul's traffic with the religious authorities of the Christian community in Jerusalem concerns the dispute at Antioch (Gal. 2:11–14) and the council in Jerusalem (Acts 15:6–29). As Luke's own traditions implied (Acts 15:39), we will argue that this dispute occurred as a result of, and therefore after, the Apostolic Council described in Acts 15, not that the dispute occurred before, and hence was resolved by, that council. Other correlations between events recorded in Acts and Galatians will also be proposed, but the key argument in what follows concerns the relationship between the Apostolic Council and its decree, and the apostolic dispute in Antioch that Paul reports. It is principally on that point, not the other possible correlations, that the argument turns.

1

THE PROBLEM

JEWISH CHRISTIANS AND GENTILE CHRISTIANS

Among the threats to the unity of the early Christian community, one of the earliest, and surely one of the most decisive, concerned the relationship between Christians of Jewish and Christians of gentile birth. It is a problem that is evident, if only in implied form, in much of the New Testament, but nowhere is it so obvious as in Paul's letter to the churches in Galatia, and in the Book of Acts. In these two documents, which along with possible references in other New Testament writings constitute our only sources of historical information about this issue, the problem poses itself frequently in terms of the relationship between Paul and the Christian authorities in Jerusalem. There is a further dimension to this problem, however, which adds to its complexity. Not only is this relationship between Paul and Jerusalem a question of the status of gentile converts, it is in addition part of a larger problem with which the Jewish people as a whole had to deal, namely, the question of how many ancestral customs could be compromised, or abandoned, in the face of the necessity of functioning as part of a Roman province.

Therefore, while the problem in the New Testament documents concerned the relationship of Jewish to gentile converts to Christianity, Paul's relationship with Jerusalem was more a problem between Jews who had become Christians than a problem between Jews and Gentiles. The issue at base was Jewish identity that expressed itself in Torah faithfulness.[1] For that reason, a twofold peril is constantly on the horizon of the events that underlie the accounts in Galatians and

4

Acts and that adds complexity to the problem and limits the avenues open to a viable solution. That twofold peril was, on the one hand, the loss of Jewish identity on the part of the Jewish Christians, with the subsequent problem of their ongoing relationship with those Jews who sought to maintain the ancestral religion without bringing down upon themselves the wrath of the Roman Empire. On the other hand, there was the division of the Christian community into Jewish and gentile parts, with the subsequent danger that, should that division become permanent, any pretense that the church was able to unite in itself all peoples would be irrevocably lost.[2] Despite the evident desire of both parties—those who found their leaders in Paul and missionaries like him and those who looked to Jerusalem for their Christian leadership—to find an acceptable *modus vivendi*, the root difficulty may well have been that each side was preoccupied with a different aspect of their relationship. The preoccupation of the leadership of the Jerusalem church may well have been with one aspect of that problem: remaining in contact with the non-Christian Jews, whatever that might require of gentile converts. Paul's overriding concern, on the other hand, may well have been with the other aspect: the problem of a division within the church into mutually exclusive Jewish and gentile parts if the demands imposed upon gentile Christians by such continuing contact with non-Christian Jews were to be theologically unacceptable.

THE ACCOUNTS OF ACTS
AND GALATIANS

The concern of Paul with respect to the unity of the church, and more specifically in terms of the recognition of the gentile Christians as legitimate members of that community in no way inferior to those of Jewish lineage, finds its concrete expression in terms of Paul's relationship to the leaders of the church in Jerusalem. That relationship, in turn, is displayed in greatest detail in the accounts found in Galatians and Acts which describe the various occasions at which the problems of unity between gentile and Jewish Christians were directly addressed. Most striking of those are two meetings, the one portrayed in Acts 15 (popularly known as the "Apostolic Council"), the other described in Galatians 2. Both meetings addressed the same problem, although in different ways and with different results. The first question we confront, therefore, one which has profound implications for both the theological and the historical dimensions of our problem, is whether or not the two accounts, one in Acts 15:1–29, the other in Gal. 2:1–10, describe or even refer to the same historic event.

Although this is as much a question of history as theology, it will not be necessary to enter into the question of an absolute chronology in relation to these accounts, since the adequacy of such a chronology is irrelevant to this question. Such chronology is necessary only when one must relate a series of events to another series of unrelated events, which is not the case here. Our question is primarily a matter of the order of a series of events, all of which occurred within the early Christian community; knowing absolute dates would help only if we could have reliable dates for the whole series of events. Given the nature of our data, with their vague references to intervals between events, the ability to determine some specific date for one of the events referred to in either of the two passages (Acts or Galatians) would not enable us to fix with any certainty the dates of other events in the sequence. For that reason, it will suffice for us to be concerned with relative rather than absolute chronology, and we will limit ourselves to the effort to solve only the sequence of events rather than the absolute dates when that sequence may have happened.[3]

To turn to the question of the relationship between the narratives in Acts and Galatians 1—2 is immediately to be involved in the tangle of problems about the nature of the narrative in Acts and the reliability of what Paul reports in Galatians. Paul's report of his two visits (Gal. 1:18–19; 2:1–10)[4] occurs in a kind of polemical context that makes the presence of argumentative bias a real possibility. The reports in Acts that concern Paul's visits to Jerusalem are cast in such general agreement with Luke's tendency to see the whole of the primitive church subservient to the apostles in Jerusalem that one is at once confronted with the real possibility that the history has been reported in such a way as to agree with what are basically theological suppositions about the way the early church developed. As though all of that were not enough, there is in addition the problem of the relationship of the two accounts of a general meeting between Paul and (some of) the apostles—the one in Acts, the other in Galatians—to each other. The problem here is that each of the narratives purports to discuss the entire history of Paul's relationship with Jerusalem, yet the two accounts disagree!

In light of the problems posed by the kind of accounts we possess of Paul's visits to Jerusalem, it can seem both daunting, and perhaps even of questionable value, to attempt to achieve any kind of reliable understanding of the historical events that underlie these narratives. Yet the events of the earliest Christian community are so important for our comprehension of the development of the church and its theology —such attempts in other areas of that development have proven valuable in both historical and theological insight[5]—that these attempts must continue to be made to achieve ever higher degrees of historical understanding. It is such an attempt upon which we must embark.

To be possible, such an attempt must make some assumptions about the nature of our evidence, and to be credible, those assumptions must be clear from the outset. Traditionally, the assumption that has been made in relation to the solution of this problem has taken the form of assigning historical priority to the narratives found in the Book of Acts, since they have been put in the form of a more elaborate narrative and chronological scheme, and hence appear to be based on more complete data. The material in Paul's own letters is then incorporated into that framework. This method of procedure is analogous to the once common practice of giving priority to the framework of John's Gospel when one sought to write an account of the career of Jesus, because the Fourth Gospel presumed a career of greater duration (perhaps up to three years); one then simply sought to fit the Synoptic accounts into it. Using this method, one employs as one's basic framework the narratives in Acts, and supplies details from Paul that are not found in that larger framework.

This practice has not gone unchallenged as a method for working with Paul and Acts any more than it has gone unchallenged working with the career of Jesus. It had already been called into question by the fourth decade of this century.[6] A few years later John Knox made perhaps the most persuasive case to date for the reverse of the more usual procedure, namely, the priority of the evidence from Paul over that from Acts.[7] Assent is now widely given to that priority,[8] although it is by no means unanimous assent.[9] While there can be little doubt that neither Paul nor Acts contains an unbiased account of what they narrate, priority must nevertheless be given, we want to urge, to the earlier narrative that was written by a participant in the events narrated, namely, to the Pauline account in Galatians.

In addition to the general problem of where priority is to be laid, with Acts or with Paul's letters, there is the more specific problem of the relationship between the narratives in Galatians, especially chapters 1—2 which detail *two* visits to Jerusalem, and the narratives in Acts 9—15, which detail *three* such visits. Some have assigned the problem to Acts, arguing that the number of visits to Jerusalem differs because the trip reported in Acts 9 simply did not occur,[10] or because the journeys reported in Acts 11 and 15 are two reports of the same visit.[11] Others have assigned the problem to Galatians, suggesting that the difference in number of visits is due to Paul having omitted a report of a visit he may well have made to Jerusalem between the two mentioned in Gal. 1:24 and 2:1; Paul would have omitted mention of it because it was not material to his argument.[12] Other possibilities have been noted and summarized by Stein,[13] Talbert,[14] and Beck,[15] among others. There is further disagreement on how one is to understand the relationship of the journey reported in Gal. 2:1–10 to the various journeys reported in Acts. The most common suggestion is to regard Gal. 2:1–10 and Acts 15:1–29 as reporting the same events, and hence the same visit,[16] although that identification of visits is also not without its problems, as John Knox pointed out.[17]

However these problems are to be resolved, and their proposed resolution is the agenda of this book, any attempt to regain an account of the historical events underlying the canonical evidence in Galatians and Acts cannot, if it is to be credible, be achieved by the simple expedient of harmonizing the two accounts. Günther Bornkamm was surely right when he wrote that an uncritical use of the material in one of the sources, whether Acts or Paul, to fill in the gaps of the other source results in something that is less than persuasive. He concludes that "combining and harmonizing [the sources] have been disastrous."[18]

Nor can one account for the differences simply on the basis of the differing points of view of the two narrators, with Paul, for example, reflecting his personal point of view, while Luke reflects the ideal of unity held by the church in the second century.[19] In such a procedure, the temptation often proves irresistible to ignore the points of real difference between the two sources in favor of a general picture whose elements have been drawn now from one, now from the other of the sources, under the assumption, for example, that Gal. 2:1–10 and Acts 15 do in fact reflect the same meeting, and that they differ only in the details each has chosen to report and the emphases each has chosen to make. As scholars have pointed out, however, the contradictions in the two accounts are simply too crass for such a procedure to prove satisfactory.[20]

Again, the problems contained in the differing accounts cannot be resolved by calling upon the probable sources Luke used in writing

Acts, with the apparent repetitions in Luke's work being due to his combination of various earlier reports.[21] Aside from the notorious difficulty scholars have experienced in attempting to identify those sources, such a solution ignores the theological tendencies at work in Acts, which on any theory of sources must take priority since they are due precisely to the author who used and shaped those sources. One can, of course, finally resolve the problem by denying its existence in the name of sound scholarship, but that is a way that has found little favor among contemporary scholars who look carefully at the evidence.[22]

The sources at our disposal—Acts and Galatians—stand on any cogent reading, in contradiction to one another,[23] not only in the number of visits of Paul to Jerusalem they relate, but also in the content and outcome of those visits. As a result, any attempt to recover the historical events underlying those accounts by means of the expedient of eliminating or even softening those contradictions by harmonizing the two accounts would thereby forfeit any claim to credibility.

PROCEDURE

Our procedure will therefore be the following. We will first survey the appropriate materials found in Acts and in Paul, in order to locate and identify that evidence that is relevant to our concern: Paul's relationship with the authorities in the early Jerusalem church. We shall look first at Acts (chap. 2) and then at Paul (chap. 3). We shall then need to resolve the problem posed by that material: We possess two bodies of evidence which tell of Paul's traffic with Jerusalem and with the authorities resident there, the one related in Acts, the other in Galatians (and in anticipatory fashion in Romans). Both purport to give complete accounts of that traffic, but they do not agree with one another either in broad outline or in specific detail (chap. 4). With that resolution proposed, we shall next undertake to account (given the nature of the evidence Luke[24] apparently had as he set his hand to compile his narrative) for the present configuration of Luke's second volume—the Book of Acts (chap. 5).

On the basis of that preparation, we shall then propose a reconstruction of the history that gave birth to the narratives as we now possess them (chap. 6). That will allow us to point out some of the implications of that reconstruction for our understanding of the course of the history of the early church (chap. 7). We will then be able to sketch out the different picture that emerges from our analysis of the New Testament materials. Finally, we will reflect on the continuing theological usefulness of the narrative in Acts, given its questionable value as a source of chronologically reliable or sequentially accurate historical information (chap. 8). In a final chapter we will point to the kind of reassessment of traditional views about early church unity and the career of the apostle Paul that our conclusions force upon us. Three appendixes that deal with problems only tangentially related to our investigation conclude the book.

2
THE EVIDENCE IN ACTS

Our task now is to locate and identify the evidence in Acts that is relevant to our concern, namely, Paul's relationship with the authorities in the early Jerusalem church, and all that that relationship entailed. We obviously cannot recount all the evidence—in too many instances that would be to retell the entire story as it appears in Acts. Rather, we shall be guided in our reflections by the importance of the various pieces of evidence for the problem with which we are concerned. As we shall see, this will be a rather straightforward procedure.

There are in Acts records of two conferences in Jerusalem where decisions were made about the relationship between Jewish legal restrictions and the gentile Christian mission. The first of those accounts is found in Acts 11, the second in Acts 15.

ACTS 11

The conference in Acts 11 was the result of Peter's mission to the Gentile Cornelius, and it was called when news reached the people in "Judea" that "the Gentiles also had received the word of God" (Acts 11:1).

> Now the apostles and the brethren who were in Judea heard that the Gentiles also had received the word of God. So when Peter went up to Jerusalem, the circumcision party criticized him, saying, "Why did you go to uncircumcised men and eat with them?" But Peter began and explained to them in order: "I was in the city of Joppa praying; and in a trance I saw a vision, something descending, like a great sheet, let down from heaven by four corners; and it came down to me. Looking at it closely I observed animals and beasts of prey and reptiles and birds of the air. And I heard a voice saying to me, 'Rise, Peter; kill and eat.' But I said

11

'No, Lord: for nothing common or unclean has ever entered my mouth.'
But the voice answered a second time from heaven, 'What God has
cleansed you must not call common.' This happened three times, and all
was drawn up again into heaven. At that very moment, three men arrived at the house in which we were, sent to me from Caesarea. And the
Spirit told me to go with them without hesitation. These six brethren
also accompanied me, and we entered the man's house. And he told us
how he had seen the angel standing in his house and saying, 'Send to
Joppa and bring Simon called Peter; he will declare to you a message by
which you will be saved, you and all your household.' As I began to
speak, the Holy Spirit fell on them just as on us at the beginning. And I
remembered the word of the Lord, how he said, 'John baptized with
water, but you shall be baptized with the Holy Spirit.' If then God gave
the same gift to them as he gave to us when we believed in the Lord Jesus
Christ, who was I that I could withstand God?" When they heard this
they were silenced. And they glorified God, saying, "Then to the Gentiles also God has granted repentance unto life."

(Acts 11:1–18)

Several points are worth noting here. This is a shorter account, in
the form of a recital, of the event itself, recorded in Acts 10. Such repetitions, though surprising when they come in such close proximity,
are in accord with ancient narrative practices, and can be observed re-
peatedly in the Old Testament and in Acts. As a result of Peter's traffic
with the Gentile Cornelius, he comes under criticism from a group
here identified as the "circumcision party." This group is never specifically defined by Luke, although it was obviously made up of people
who felt no intimate social intercourse could take place with uncircumcised people. Although Luke does not say so, it is almost certain
that we are to understand them as Jews who have become Christians,
and who felt that non-Jews had first to be circumcised, that is, become
Jews, before they could become Christians. As Peter's vision implies,
the crux of the issue was table fellowship, where a Jew would most
quickly become polluted in a non-kosher atmosphere. Peter's account
of his vision, which had as its point doing away with the dietary restrictions essential to any conception of "kosher" foods, is then accepted by the "circumcision party." Their conclusion, which consis-
ted of glorifying God for spreading the acceptance of the gospel
("repentance unto life") beyond the bounds of the Jewish law, indeed
with doing away with that part of the law that restricted table fellowship, clearly implies their acceptance that Gentiles could now become
Christians without first becoming Jews and undergoing circumcision.

12

In light of this, it would not be out of place to assume that, as the account now stands, we are to understand that no restrictions were to be placed upon gentile converts, since the Holy Spirit had fallen on Cornelius and those of his household just as it had fallen on the disciples at the time of Pentecost. The important point for our purposes is that we have in Acts 11 a conference where Peter played a leading role and where there was agreement that no restrictions were to be laid upon gentile converts to the Christian faith.

ACTS 15

A second conference is recorded in Acts 15.[1] It resulted from the announcement "by some who came down from Judea" to Antioch, by that time a center of the gentile mission, that unless one followed Mosaic customs (i.e., the law, including circumcision), one could not be saved (Acts 15:1). As a result of "no small dissension and debate" about this claim (v. 2a), a delegation that included Paul and Barnabas was sent from Antioch to Jerusalem to discuss this matter (15:2b–4). When they arrived, they were faced with the same assertion, this time from Christian Pharisees: Circumcision and keeping the law of Moses were necessary for Christians, Gentiles included. The account of the ensuing conference is given in Acts 15:6–21:

> The apostles and the elders were gathered together to consider this matter. And after there had been much debate, Peter rose and said to them, "Brethren, you know that in the early days God made choice among you, that by my mouth the Gentiles should hear the word of the gospel and believe. And God who knows the heart bore witness to them, giving them the Holy Spirit just as he did to us; and he made no distinction between us and them, but cleansed their hearts by faith. Now therefore why do you make trial of God by putting a yoke upon the neck of the disciples which neither our fathers nor we have been able to bear? But we believe that we shall be saved through the grace of the Lord Jesus, just as they will."
>
> And all the assembly kept silence; and they listened to Barnabas and Paul as they related what signs and wonders God had done through them among the Gentiles. After they finished speaking, James replied, "Brethren, listen to me. Symeon has related how God first visited the Gentiles, to take out of them a people for his name. And with this the words of the prophets agree, as it is written, 'After this I will return, and I will rebuild the dwelling of David, which has fallen; I will rebuild its ruins, and I will set it up, that the rest of men may seek the Lord, and all the Gentiles who are called by my name, says the Lord, who has made these things known

from of old.' Therefore my judgment is that we should not trouble those of the Gentiles who turn to God, but should write to them to abstain from the pollutions of idols (*alisgematōn tōn eidōlōn*) and from unchastity (*porneias*) and from what is strangled (*pniktou*) and from blood (*aimatos*). For from early generations Moses has had in every city those who preach him, for he is read every sabbath in the synagogues."

The decision expressed by James, that certain minimum legal requirements were to be observed by gentile converts, was then agreed upon by "the whole church" (v. 22) and included in a letter sent by "the brethren, both the apostles and the elders" (v. 23), and delivered by Paul, Barnabas, Judas Barsabbas, and Silas, "leading men among the brethren" (v. 22). In that letter, the legal requirements are given: "abstain from what has been sacrificed to idols (*eidōlothytōn*) and from blood (*aimatos*) and from what is strangled (*pnikton*) and from unchastity (*porneias*)."[2] Thus we have in Acts 15 a conference where James played a leading role and where restrictions were laid upon Gentile converts.

THE APOSTOLIC DECREE

It must also be noted that there is another account that includes mention of the Apostolic Decree, namely, Acts 21:25, where James informs Paul that he, James, has sent a letter with his judgment that gentile Christians should observe that decree. The wording of the decree James recites agrees with the wording in the letter mentioned in Acts 15:29 rather than with James's original proposal in 15:20:

> But as for the Gentiles who have believed, we have sent a letter with our judgment that they should abstain from what has been sacrificed to idols (*eidōlothyton*) and from blood (*aima*) and from what is strangled (*pnikton*) and from unchastity (*porneia*).
>
> (Acts 21:25)

What is remarkable is that this announcement is made to Paul as though he were hearing the decree for the first time, despite the fact that according to Acts 15:22, he not only participated in the conference that produced it but was also included in the delegation that delivered the letter containing the decree to a number of churches. The discrepancy is not easy to explain. We find unconvincing the suggestion that this latter reference in Acts 21 is for the benefit of Acts' readers, rather than being a part of the narrative and thus intended for the information of the characters in it, in this case Paul.[3] Ernst Haenchen suggests that such remarks are a common device in Acts,[4] but the one example he cites, Acts 1:18–20, is irrelevant in this context since it contains information not heretofore given the reader in Acts up to that point, whereas the material in 21:25 has been given not only once but twice before. There is, furthermore, no indication in the text of the narrative that the author of Acts intended the remark in 21:25 for his readers rather than as part of his narrative.[5] In the context of Acts 21, there is no hint that Paul is not learning of this letter for the first time. In fact, Acts has no such remarks directed clearly to the reader at all, and the narrative is quite self-contained, with no asides by the narrator to interrupt the narrative flow (for such asides, see Mark 13:14, "Let the reader understand"; or Mark 13:37, "And what I say to you I say to all: Watch").

If anything, Acts 21:25 is more firmly anchored in its context than either of the other two lists of the four prohibitions imposed on the Gentiles.[6] It can thus be argued that 21:25, far from being an unfortunate redactional insert,[7] in fact represents the original tradition and thus is the source for the material about the decree in 15:20 and 29.[8] Corroborative evidence may be gathered from scholars who have concluded from the evidence in Paul's *own* letters that he cannot have been present when the decree was formulated.[9]

THE EVENTS ACCORDING TO ACTS

Two further elements in the report of the "Apostolic Conference" contained in Acts 15 are useful to note in this context. First, although Barnabas and Paul are said to have given a report of their work, no content of that speech is given:

> And all the assembly kept silence; and they listened to Barnabas and Paul as they related what signs and wonders God had done through them among the Gentiles.
>
> (Acts 15:12)

In addition, the report is completely ignored from that point on. When James speaks subsequently, he makes no reference to Barnabas and Paul, and what he says bears much closer resemblance to Peter's experience with Cornelius (Acts 10; summarized in 15:7–9 [see above]) than to anything reported in the interim about the conference. It therefore appears very much as though Luke inserted the reference to Barnabas and Paul in 15:12b[10] into an account of an event where they were not originally present.[11]

There is a second element worthy of note in the report of the Apostolic Conference in Acts 15: James responds to a speech given by Peter, but designates him as "Symeon," a name Peter carries nowhere else in Acts. Who this Symeon is has been a matter of some conjecture. Many have argued that this is simply the Aramaic form of Simon Peter's name, as in 2 Pet. 1:1.[12] There are, however, other men named "Symeon" in the New Testament, among them an ancestor of Jesus (Luke 3:30), and the prophet Symeon (Luke 2:25–34). John Chrysostom thought the latter was the one to whom James referred at the Apostolic Council.[13] There is also a Symeon in Acts, but he is Symeon Niger, one of the "prophets and teachers" at Antioch (13:1) whom Luke mentions along with Barnabas, Saul (= Paul), and some others.[14] We shall return to this matter later.

At the conclusion of the council, four people were commissioned to deliver the letter containing the decree: Paul, Barnabas, Judas Barsabbas, and Silas. The account of the delivery is in Acts 15:30–35:

> So when they were sent off, they went down to Antioch; and having gathered the congregation together, they delivered the letter. And when they read it, they rejoiced at the exhortation. And Judas and Silas, who were themselves prophets, exhorted the brethren with many words and strengthened them. And after they had spent some time, they were sent off in peace by the brethren to those who had sent them. But Paul and Barnabas remained in Antioch, teaching and preaching the word of the Lord, with many others also.

It is interesting to note that although four were commissioned to deliver the letter, only two, Judas and Silas, are mentioned as reporting the content and apparently urging compliance. That is all the more remarkable since Barnabas and Paul had been specifically commissioned by the congregation in Antioch to get the matter cleared up (15:2); one would then naturally have expected them to report on the outcome on their return. Instead, we hear only of Judas and Silas making such a report, and then returning to Jerusalem when their task was finished. The lack of any mention of Paul and Barnabas reporting the outcome of their commission seems again, therefore, to be an indication that their names were added as participants in an event in which they actually did not share.

Two further events reported in Acts are worthy of note before we turn to a consideration of the evidence contained in Paul's letters. The first event is a sharp dissension that arose between Paul and Barnabas in Antioch, after the Apostolic Council. It is reported in Acts 15:36–40:

> And after some days Paul said to Barnabas, "Come, let us return and visit the brethren in every city where we proclaimed the word of the Lord, and see how they are." And Barnabas wanted to take with them John called Mark. But Paul thought best not to take with them one who had withdrawn from them in Pamphylia, and had not gone with them to the work. And there arose a sharp contention, so that they separated from each other; Barnabas took Mark with him and sailed away to Cyprus, but Paul chose Silas and departed, being commended by the brethren to the grace of the Lord.

The disagreement between Paul and Barnabas centered, according to this account, on disagreement about whether to take John Mark on another journey after he had deserted them on an earlier one (see Acts 13:13). Barnabas then did take John Mark, and Paul chose Silas, even though the last we heard of him, he had returned to Jerusalem after delivering the letter containing the Apostolic Decree (15:33). Either this is a different Silas, or else Luke had no information about his subsequent return to Antioch. In any case, the separation of Paul and Barnabas reported here in Acts reflects a split in the gentile mission that centered in Antioch, a split that occurred at some time subsequent to the Apostolic Council.[15]

The second event reported in Acts that needs to be mentioned in this context is the trip Barnabas and Paul (there still called "Saul") made to Jerusalem during a period of worldwide famine which had been foretold by Agabus and which, Luke tells us, occurred in the fifth decade of the first century. It is reported in Acts 11:27–30:

> Now in these days prophets came down from Jerusalem to Antioch. And one of them named Agabus stood up and foretold by the Spirit that there would be a great famine over all the world; and this took place in the days of Claudius. And the disciples determined, every one according to his ability, to send relief to the brethren who lived in Judea; and they did so, sending it to the elders by the hand of Barnabas and Saul.

Acts is quite specific about this famine, noting that it occurred in the time of the Roman emperor Claudius, whose rule spanned the years A.D. 41–54. Despite that appearance of historical veracity, we possess no other records to indicate any such worldwide famine during that decade and a half.[16] In a rough parallel to the case of the second men-

17

tion of the Apostolic Decree in 21:25, there is also a second reference, recorded in Acts 24:17, to an offering brought by Paul to Jerusalem ("Now after some years I came to bring to my nation alms and offerings"), this time in the context of Paul's speech to the Roman governor Felix about Paul's arrest during what proved to be his final visit to Jerusalem.

These references to the two offerings brought by Paul to Jerusalem represent a major discrepancy between the narratives of Paul's visits there in Acts and in Galatians. Attempts to harmonize that discrepancy only tend to demonstrate its utter intractability, as some examples will show. Martin Hengel: "Luke does not always say everything that he knows;"[17] that is, that is why he does not mention this as the reason for Paul's final visit to Jerusalem in Acts 19:21 ("Now after these events Paul resolved in the Spirit to pass through Macedonia and Achaia and go to Jerusalem, saying, 'After I have been there, I must also see Rome'"). Keith Nickle: a "double allusion" is to be understood in Gal. 2:10, one to a past famine visit, and one to the impending collection, the earlier visit revealed by the past tense at the end of that statement ("Only they would have us remember the poor, which very thing I *was eager* to do" [emphasis mine]).[18] Stanley Toussaint: Paul did not report the earlier famine visit in Galatians 1—2 because he "did not see any apostles" on that visit, "he only saw elders."[19] John Knox was probably correct on this point when he maintained that Luke's view that the settlement of the Jewish-Christian dispute occurred early in Paul's missionary career (after Paul's "first missionary journey," at the time of the Apostolic Council) left no place for a peace offering to be brought to Jerusalem at the end of Paul's career.[20] However one may want to resolve the discrepancy, it is clear that this reference in Acts 24:17 is to Paul's final visit to Jerusalem, and the offering is mentioned in a way that makes it appear to have been the reason for that visit and for his subsequent arrest. That is the only reference in Acts to that later offering, however.

RESULTS

Our survey of the evidence in Luke related to Paul's contacts with Jerusalem relative to the question of the relationship between Jewish and gentile Christians has produced the following results: There was a conference where Peter played a key role and where there was agreement that no restrictions were to be laid upon gentile converts to the Christian faith (Acts 11:1–18). There was, in addition, a conference where James played a key role and where restrictions were laid upon gentile converts (Acts 15:6–21), those restrictions being conveyed by means of a letter carried by Paul, among others. There was a second report of those restrictions, a report delivered by James to Paul, but in a narrative context framed as though Paul had known nothing about them prior to that conversation.

There was, further, a report of a visit by Paul (and Barnabas) to Jerusalem in order to bring famine relief (11:27–30). There was also a report of a second visit by Paul to Jerusalem in order to bring "alms and offerings," a visit during which he was arrested. There was no prior hint in Acts, however, that an offering was the reason for that last visit. Finally, we learned that at some point after the Apostolic Council there was a sharp dispute between Paul and Barnabas which resulted in their separation from each other in their missionary endeavors, evidently causing a split in the gentile mission that was headquartered in Antioch.

3

THE EVIDENCE IN PAUL

When we turn to Paul, to investigate the evidence relating to his relationship with the Jewish-Christian authorities in Jerusalem, we are restricted primarily to the accounts in the first two chapters of his letter to the Christians in Galatia, with one or two other passages in other letters which serve to corroborate what is said in Galatians.

GALATIANS

Paul reports only two visits to Jerusalem in his letter to the Galatians. He also refers to a third contact with the Jerusalem authorities, but this time in the form of contact with their representatives who had been sent to Antioch. In his description of his two visits to Jerusalem (Gal. 1:18—2:10), Paul specifically denies any visit prior to the first of the two he reports:

> But when he who had set me apart before I was born, and had called me through his grace, was pleased to reveal his Son to me, in order that I might preach him among the Gentiles, I did not confer with flesh and blood, nor did I go up to Jerusalem to those who were apostles before me, but I went away into Arabia; and again I returned to Damascus.
>
> (Gal. 1:15–17)

In that context in Galatians, the point of Paul's denial was evidently to forestall the allegation that he had sought or received any kind of authoritative corroboration or interpretation of his call to evangelize the Gentiles.[1]

First Visit to Jerusalem

The first of Paul's two visits to Jerusalem is reported in Gal. 1:18–23:

20

THE EVIDENCE IN PAUL

Then after three years I went up to Jerusalem to visit Cephas, and remained with him fifteen days. But I saw none of the other apostles except
James the Lord's brother. (In what I am writing to you, before God, I do
not lie!) Then I went into the regions of Syria and Cilicia. And I was still
not known by sight to the churches of Christ in Judea; they only heard it
said, "He who once persecuted us is now preaching the faith he once tried
to destroy." And they glorified God because of me.

This visit, which occurred three years after Paul's conversion (see
1:15–17) and which lasted two weeks,[2] involved contact with only
two disciples, Peter in the primary role, and somewhat secondarily,
James. The oath of veracity gives an indication that some either did
not accept that account, or were giving a different account of Paul's
relationship to Jerusalem and his visits there. While the Greek verb
translated "to visit" (*historein*) is more formal than the conduct implied
in the English, and carries an implication of "finding out about or
from,"[3] there is no question here of any kind of consultation with the
apostles and elders in Jerusalem, or even with a group of the apostles.
Nor is there any hint that any kind of decision was reached here relating to the gentile Christian mission, or to the relationship between
gentile and Jewish Christians. While Peter and Paul will have done
more during the "visit" than talk about the weather[4]—it is probable
that during that time, Paul will have questioned Peter about the life
and teachings of Jesus—it is clear that the visit was not in any sense a
consultation with the apostles in Jerusalem. On that the reader has
Paul's oath (v. 20).

Second Visit to Jerusalem

Galatians 2:1–10 offers a somewhat fuller account relating to Paul's
second visit to Jerusalem:

Then after fourteen years I went up again to Jerusalem with Barnabas,
taking Titus along with me. I went up by revelation; and I laid before
them (but privately before those who were of repute) the gospel which I
preach among the Gentiles, lest somehow I should be running or had run
in vain. But even Titus, who was with me, was not compelled to be circumcised, though he was a Greek. But because of false brethren secretly
brought in, who slipped in to spy out our freedom which we have in
Christ Jesus, that they might bring us to bondage—to them we did not
yield submission even for a moment, that the truth of the gospel might
be preserved for you. And from those who were reputed to be something
(what they were makes no difference to me, God shows no partiality)—

21

those, I say, who were of repute added nothing to me; but on the contrary, when they saw that I had been entrusted with the gospel to the uncircumcised, just as Peter had been entrusted with the gospel to the circumcised (for he who worked through Peter for the mission to the circumcised worked through me also for the Gentiles), and when they perceived the grace that was given to me, James and Cephas and John, who were reputed to be pillars, gave to me and Barnabas the right hand of fellowship, that we should go to the Gentiles and they to the circumcised; only they would have us remember the poor, which very thing I was eager to do (*ho kai espoudasa auto touto poiēsai*).

It is not clear whether the point of origin for the fourteen years was the conversion or the first visit to Jerusalem. Taking into account the inclusive reckoning current in Paul's time, the visit was thirteen years after either his conversion or his earlier visit to Jerusalem. In either case, sufficient time had elapsed for Paul to have established a number of churches among the Gentiles, and thus to have established his credentials as a Christian missionary; that seems to be the point to be taken from this rather long interval between visits (either thirteen or ten years). At this second meeting, there was a consultation between Paul and the three "pillar apostles,"[5] a consultation which was concerned specifically with Paul's proclamation of the Christian faith among the Gentiles.

There has been considerable discussion about whether or not Paul went to Jerusalem to seek confirmation of his gospel from the apostles there, particularly in light of his repeated affirmation of independence from those Jerusalem authorities which dominates his letter to the Galatians. The most probable conclusion, I would urge, is that although Paul did not seek added authority for his preaching in the form of approbation from the authorities in Jerusalem, he did need to ascertain that the Lord he had seen was in fact the risen Jesus. Confirmation on that point would mean that his gospel was the same as the gospel of those in Jerusalem.[6] An adverse judgment on that score would have shown Paul's preaching to have been empty, as he himself suggests in 2:2.[7] The question was ultimately one of the unity of the gospel, and therefore of the church.[8]

The leading roles at this conference were played by Paul, Peter (vv. 7–8), and James (v. 9), with one reference to John as the third apostle of repute (v. 9; cf. v. 6). It is noteworthy that in this account of the conference, the Greek name "Peter" appears in vv. 7–8, as opposed to Paul's more usual Aramaic "Kephas" (e.g., 1:18; 2:9, 11; 1 Cor. 9:6,

15:5). Some have suggested that the presence in this passage of the Greek name reflects Paul's use here of an official (Greek) document which emerged from that meeting.[9] It would seem strange that a meeting in Jerusalem would have its "minutes" framed in Greek, however. Others have suggested that Paul used the Greek form here because he wanted to emphasize the central authority of Peter,[10] but unless Paul has in mind a passage like Matt. 16:18, improbable in the extreme, it is hard to see why the Greek name would convey more authority than the Aramaic. Whatever one may decide on that issue, the appearance of James as first in the list of the three pillar apostles may well mean that by this time James had assumed the central rule in the church in Jerusalem.[11] But Paul's own report here in Galatians, singling out Peter as having missionary authority, shows that for him at least Peter played the central role along with Paul himself in this conference. Being entrusted with the gospel to the circumcised would surely constitute greater importance for Paul than presiding over the church in Jerusalem at that time.

The outcome of this conference (at the time Paul was writing Galatians, reports about it were evidently circulating[12]) was the agreement that Paul was to "remember the poor,"[13] evidently in the form of an offering. Paul's expressed willingness to do that (given in the aorist forms of the verbs: *espoudasa* and *poiēsai*) has led some to suggest that we may infer that Paul was referring to a continuing activity, thus implying that the famine visit of Acts 11 had already taken place.[14] Yet Paul's narrative is told as happening in the past, and the aorist *espoudasa* (2:10) may have no more significance than that (tenses of infinitives [*poiēsai*] do not in any case imply time of occurrence).

There is no further mention in Paul's account of any other agreement with respect to this conference relating to the gentile mission, whether in the matters of circumcision, ritual, or dietary or ethical rules. While some have argued, on the basis of Paul's convoluted language in 2:3, that Titus was in fact circumcised as a result of this conference,[15] one must question such a conclusion particularly in the light of the total context of Paul's argument in Galatians 1—2.[16] Nor is there any reference, even an oblique one, to the Apostolic Decree of Acts 15, or of any kind of agreement that would represent even the roughest kind of approximation to it.[17] The outcome of the conference was the agreement that Paul would "remember the poor," and that was all! From the report in Galatians 2, we have no reason to believe that Paul was not quite satisfied with the outcome of that meeting in Jerusalem. He had come to Jerusalem to see whether his apostolic mission was valid and had evidently heard nothing to the contrary. Indeed, the language of the report in Galatians makes clear that it was recognized by the three pillar apostles as valid.[18]

In Gal. 2:1–10, therefore, we have a report on a second visit by Paul to Jerusalem where he struck an agreement with the three pillar apostles that he should carry on his mission to the Gentiles while they carried on a mission to the Jews. The only condition laid upon Paul was that he take an offering for the poor, a condition he gladly assumed. There is no mention here of any further restriction to be laid either upon Paul in the conduct of the mission, or upon gentile Christians. From his own account, it would seem that Paul was satisfied with the outcome of the meeting.

Conference in Antioch

Paul's dissatisfaction with the authorities in Jerusalem, and with Peter as one of them, occurred during a subsequent meeting in Antioch where Paul, Barnabas, and Peter were present. It is recorded in Gal. 2:11–13:

> But when Cephas came to Antioch I opposed him to his face, because he stood condemned. For before certain men came from James, he ate with the Gentiles; but when they came he drew back and separated himself, fearing the circumcision party. And with him the rest of the Jews acted insincerely, so that even Barnabas was carried away by their insincerity.

The reason for Peter's presence in Antioch is not stated, although it seems clear from the account that Peter was the visitor in the place while Paul was accustomed to being there. That would not be surprising since Antioch was the home base of the gentile mission. There is also no indication of the time interval between the meeting in Jerusalem between Paul, on the one hand, and James, Peter, and John on the other, and this visit by Peter to Antioch, nor of the interval between Peter's arrival and that of the "men from James." Whatever the reason may have been for Peter's visit —perhaps a courtesy call, or a stopover on one of his missionary journeys, or even an attempt to convert Jews living in Antioch—the reason for the visit of the "men from James" is clear enough: They brought a message which resulted in the withdrawal of Christian Jews from table fellowship with Christian Gentiles.

What that message was we are given no hint. It is clear, however, that as men "from" (probably "sent by") James, they belonged to the circumcision party. Whether or not they are the same as the circumcision party of Acts 11:2 or those described in 15:2 (who claimed that "unless you are circumcised according to the custom of Moses, you cannot be saved") is not clear, but that they represented the same outlook found in the church in Jerusalem is clear enough. The "false brethren" Paul mentions in Gal. 2:4 who apparently failed to compel Titus to be circumcised (2:3) may also have belonged to the same party. But whether they did or not, they too represented the same theological orientation within the Jerusalem church.

Although the content of the message is not given, its upshot is clear enough, namely, the breaking-off of table fellowship between Jewish and gentile Christians which apparently to that time had been undertaken as a matter of course. Peter had obviously also shared in that fellowship, since Paul specifically mentions Peter's withdrawal from it when he received the message brought by the men from James.[19] So authoritative was the message that it also influenced the behavior of Barnabas. Probably because he had accompanied and presumably supported Paul in the meeting with the three pillar apostles and had shared the "right hand of fellowship" (i.e., complete agreement) with them as one who like Paul was to carry on the mission to the Gentiles, Paul laments that "*even Barnabas* was carried away by their insincerity" (emphasis mine).

That Paul regarded this breaking-off of table fellowship with gentile Christians on the part of the Jewish Christians as wrong is evident—he brands it "insincerity." Clearly he understood it as a breach of the agreement he had reached with the Jerusalem authorities, including James and Peter. Because this dispute with Peter and his actions bears directly on the problem in Galatia, Paul turns immediately in his letter to that question. We hear nothing more about his relationship with Jerusalem or the leaders there, or even with Peter or Barnabas, in the remainder of the letter to the Galatians.

We do have, however, in these verses in Galatians 2, an account of a dispute in Antioch involving Peter, Barnabas and Paul, with the upshot that Barnabas sided with those who acted insincerely. He thus shared in the wrath Paul turned against Peter (2:14–16). That wrath carries at least an implication that such activity betrayed a faulty or insufficient understanding of the implications of God's saving act in Jesus Christ. It would be fair to speak of a break at this point between Paul and Barnabas in their understanding of the relationship between the gentile mission and its converts and converts from among the Jews.

ROMANS

If there is no more information about Paul's relationship with the authorities in Jerusalem in Galatians, we do learn from Rom. 15:25–27 that Paul did plan one more visit to them:

> At present, however, I am going to Jerusalem with aid for the saints. For Macedonia and Achaia have been pleased to make some contribution for the poor among the saints at Jerusalem; they were pleased to do it, and indeed they are in debt to them, for if the Gentiles have come to share in their spiritual blessings, they ought also to be of service to them in material blessings.

From the language—the offering is "for the poor among the saints" there[20]—it seems evident that this offering is the one Paul had agreed to undertake at the time of his second visit to Jerusalem (Gal. 2:10). The omission of mention of churches from Galatia among those who have contributed is noteworthy. Perhaps the difficulties there had not been resolved in Paul's favor, or perhaps they had been unable, for whatever reason, to get the money to Paul for his trip to Jerusalem.

There is a second element of interest in Paul's report to the Roman Christians of his planned visit to Jerusalem, and that is the anticipation of trouble there:

> I appeal to you, brethren, by our Lord Jesus Christ and by the love of the Spirit, to strive together with me in your prayers to God on my behalf, that I may be delivered from the unbelievers in Judea, and that my service for Jerusalem may be acceptable to the saints.
>
> (Rom. 15:30–31)

From this language it is clear that Paul anticipated possible trouble from two sources: the one from the Jews who had not become Christians (the "unbelievers in Judea"), the other from Jews who had ("the saints"). If the troubles anticipated are of a different quality— something he needed to be delivered from, possibly physical violence on the part of the nonbelievers and rejection of his offering on the part of the believers—it is evident that Paul was aware of a dual hostility against him in Jerusalem. The possible rejection of the offering indicates that the harmony achieved at the time of his second visit to Jerusalem has since been replaced by a more antagonistic outlook toward him. As a result, Paul fears the Jerusalem authorities will no longer feel that the gesture of an offering from gentile Christians—with whatever theological overtones,it may have carried— will be appropriate at this time. That in its turn would mean that the agreement as a result of which Paul pledged to make the offering is no longer regarded by Jerusalem as valid. In such circumstances, the offering would have become a gesture of reconciliation, perhaps even a symbol that Paul still felt the agreement binding upon him, and, by inference, upon those in Jerusalem as well.

Finally, we must note that nowhere in any of Paul's accounts of his visits to Jerusalem, or in the accounts of his contacts with the authorities located there, past and projected, is there any explicit discussion of the Apostolic Decree cited in Acts. Indeed, Paul nowhere explicitly mentions it, or gives any reason to believe that he entered into any agreement with the Jerusalem authorities with respect to the gentile mission other than that he and Barnabas were to share it, and that he, Paul, would collect and deliver an offering for the poor in Jerusalem. The only condition that resulted from Paul's Apostolic Council related in Gal. 2:1–10 is that Paul remember the poor, something which in its turn is not associated anywhere in Acts with the Apostolic Council described in chapter 15.

RESULTS

Our survey of the evidence in Paul's letters concerning his contacts with Jerusalem relative to the question of the relationship between Jewish and gentile Christians has produced the following results: There was a visit by Paul to Jerusalem, where he met only two of the apostles, and one of them, James, only secondarily. At that first visit, Peter played the leading role, and no decisions were reached concerning Paul's mission or the relationship of gentile and Jewish Christians. There was a second visit by Paul to Jerusalem where he conferred with the authorities, chief among whom were James, Peter, and John, with Peter the chief apostle vis-à-vis Paul's Gentile mission. During this second visit, Paul struck an agreement with the three pillar apostles that he should carry on his mission to the Gentiles, and they the mission to the Jews. The only condition laid upon Paul was that he take an offering for the poor, a condition he gladly assumed.

There is a third account, which tells of a dispute in Antioch involving Peter, Barnabas, and Paul. That dispute resulted in a misunderstanding between Barnabas and Paul which Paul attributed to Barnabas's insincerity and lack of understanding of the implications of the

Christian faith for the relationship between Jewish and gentile Christians. Finally, Paul tells of a planned trip to Jerusalem to deliver the offering even though he anticipates trouble there from nonbelieving as well as believing Jews. Nowhere did we find any mention of the Apostolic Decree, or its contents, in relation to Paul's visits to Jerusalem.

4

THE NATURE
OF OUR EVIDENCE

We possess, as we have seen, two accounts of Paul's traffic with Jerusalem, and with the authorities resident there, the one related in Acts, the other in Galatians (and in anticipatory fashion in Romans). We have also seen that these accounts do not agree with one another, even though both purport to give complete accounts of that traffic. We must now attempt to account for this state of affairs.

PAUL'S ACCOUNTS

Once again, I want to argue that major credibility must be given to the accounts of Paul, who wrote chronologically closer to the events he narrates and who gives an account of events in which he himself was a participant. That is of course not to say that everything Paul says in Galatians 1—2 is objective information, to be assumed as representing no particular point of view and devoid of all bias.[1] Obviously, Paul is writing this letter to support his cause, to combat what he takes to be a totally false interpretation of the gospel of Jesus Christ, and to convey his understanding of the issues and their correct outcome. That is not conducive to objectivity. Furthermore, Paul's statements about his former devastation of the church, and his amazing progress in Judaism, bear some marks of exaggeration:

> For you have heard of my former life in Judaism, how I persecuted the church of God violently and tried to destroy it; and I advanced beyond many of my own age among my people, so extremely zealous was I for the traditions of my faith.
>
> (Gal. 1:13—15)

29

This attempt by Paul to show how remarkable his conversion was, and how well he understood his former religious state, touches on points of considerable importance for his ensuing discussion, and would therefore be highlighted by Paul in his own thinking on this matter.

Again, Paul's claim that he went to Jerusalem the second time "by revelation" (Gal. 2:2) neglects to tell us how that revelation was mediated. It is quite possible that an outsider might well have concluded that Paul went to Jerusalem at the instigation of some person whom Paul would have said was the one who mediated the "revelation" of God's will to him. Further, Paul's identification of his opponents as "false brethren" (*pseudadelphous*, 2:4), a title they would almost surely have reciprocated in relation to Paul, clearly portrays his "bias" in that discussion. Paul's eagerness to do just what the apostles wanted done with respect to the poor (2:10b) may also project more enthusiasm in the remembering than the others present at the meeting might have been able to detect.

On the other hand, Paul's oath precisely in relation to these events in Jerusalem (Gal. 1:20: "In what I am writing to you, before God, I do not lie [*ou pseudomai*]"): that he saw only two apostles on his first journey to Jerusalem as an apostle (1:19), lends credibility to his account, despite the attempts of some scholars to affirm that the oath is nothing but a rhetorical device. Paul's very Jewishness would have put strong restraint on any such rhetorical devices leading him to make statements falsifying his past, when as a witness for the truth of those statements he invoked the divine presence. Again, the context in which Paul placed his narrative of journeys to Jerusalem is one where falsification of any point there would also falsify all else he wanted to say to the Galatians, since those later points were tied so closely to the points he wanted to make in this narrative. Such placement therefore put further constraints on the freedom Paul could exercise in shaping his account of his visits to Jerusalem to support his argument. All of that simply meant he could not make his theological points to the Galatians irrespective of the truth of the contents of his historical narrative, lest an opponent, able to falsify a historical detail, could thereby claim to falsify Paul's theological points as well. Such constraints (oath, chance of falsification) were, so far as we can tell, not operative, at least not to the same extent, in the case of the narratives in Acts.

If, then, there were biases operative in the case of Paul, there were also constraints, both in form and content, on his narratives about his visits to Jerusalem and their outcome, constraints that would tend to annul the free play of those biases. There is the additional point that what Paul narrates are events in which he himself took part. That is not the case with respect to Acts, where the author nowhere binds himself by oath as to the truthfulness of certain details (he only claims careful attention to eyewitness traditions [Luke 1:2–3]), nor does he claim to have been a participant in, or even an observer at, the events in Jerusalem that he narrates.

LUKE'S ACCOUNTS

Since Acts, like the Gospel of Luke, gives evidence of having been assembled from a variety of sources, something to which Luke himself at least points (Luke 1:1–2), our next task is to inquire what information Luke is likely to have possessed that, given the assumptions he brought to his understanding of the early church, and given the sometimes rather different information contained in the accounts of those events we have in Galatians 1—2, would have caused him to write as he did. Our question therefore is: What kind of information did Luke possess that would have led him to give to his history the shape it now has? This inquiry will consist of two parts: First, we must investigate the information Luke apparently possessed. Then we must see how Luke's assumptions about the nature of the church and its development would have led him to shape his material into the narrative in Acts.

Luke's Information

C. K. Barrett has put the state of affairs we confront in Acts as succinctly and clearly as anyone:

> What the work of the past generations has shown beyond doubt is that Luke's narrative is patchy. It has been put together from more than one source, and though it contains material of historical value, the history can be reconstructed only if we are prepared to take to pieces the story as it stands and examine the several parts of which it is composed.[2]

While attempts have been made to find in Acts evidence of written sources, they have not evoked general agreement as to their limits or provenance. If Luke did possess them, he will have worked them over in the same way he reworked material he took from Mark for his Gospel, which is to say that he rewrote them to such an extent that they will be for all practical purposes unrecoverable. There is currently some agreement among scholars that Luke did possess and rework

31

traditions, few, if any, written, and that he did not possess the letters of Paul.[3] I want to argue that Luke was dependent upon "incomplete and conflicting reminiscences"[4] for his information about the history he wrote, and that Acts represents "Luke's selection and interpretation of [that] early data."[5]

1. It is evident in the first instance that Luke possessed information that there had been strife in the church in Antioch between gentile and Jewish Christians. Luke understood this to be the cause, for example, of the Apostolic Council portrayed in Acts 15 (cf. vv. 1–2; cf. also Gal. 1:21). Luke also possessed information that two conferences had been held in Jerusalem at which decisions were made concerning the relationship between the Jewish and gentile Christian movements (Acts 11:1–18; 15:1–29). At one of those conferences no restrictions were placed on gentile Christians (Acts 11:1–18; cf. Gal. 2:1–10). At the other restrictions were imposed (Acts 15:1–29; no parallel account in Paul).[6]

2. It is further apparent that Luke knew Peter played a prominent role in one of those conferences (Acts 11:2, 4; cf. Gal. 1:18) and that James played a prominent role in the other (Acts 15:13, 19; cf. Gal. 2:12). The similarities between the issues discussed in the councils in Jerusalem reported in Acts 11 and 15 have prompted some scholars to regard them as duplicate,[7] or at least parallel,[8] accounts. Here again, although some scholars have attempted to account for these similarities by seeking to isolate possible sources underlying one or both of these accounts,[9] many others doubt that it can be done.[10] Such scholars tend instead to attempt to discern what information Luke had, as we are doing, without trying to identify the extent or milieu of the sources.[11]

3. Luke knew, further, that Paul had been present at one of those councils (he reported Paul as present in Acts 15) but not at the other (Paul is not mentioned in Acts 11). Luke also knew of a tradition, which he apparently chose not to credit, that the conference Paul attended was not the one where decisions were made to place restrictions on gentile Christians (Acts 21:25; cf. Gal. 2:6, 10). That tradition is displayed when James reports to Paul on the letter he and others sent informing Gentiles of the Apostolic Decree, a report assuming that Paul was learning of the letter and the decree for the first time. Although Luke preserved that tradition, he nevertheless felt obliged not only to include Paul at the conference, but also to include him among those who delivered that letter in the account in Acts 15. The reason

why Luke apparently felt compelled to do this we will discuss later. Because of this report to Paul by James in Acts 21:25, as well as for other reasons, most scholars have come to hold that the Apostolic Decree was not promulgated at the council to which Acts 15 refers[12] any more than its contents could have been formulated at the conference Paul described in Gal. 2:1–10.[13]

4. Luke also knew that someone named "Symeon" had played a significant role in the conference where the decision was made to place restrictions on gentile Christians.[14]

5. Again, Luke knew that a split in the gentile Christian movement had occurred following the conference where the restrictions on the gentile Christian movement had been formulated, and that as a result Paul and Barnabas had parted company (Acts. 15:39; cf. Gal. 2:11–13).[15] Luke may also have had information that the restrictions to be imposed upon gentile Christians represented a compromise between the Jewish and gentile factions (no circumcision but some legal observances; cf. Acts 15:19–21). Clearly enough, in the framework of the dispute in Acts (15:5), the decree would represent a compromise.[16]

6. Finally, Luke knew that Paul had brought a gift of money to Jerusalem in connection with his final visit there. It is worth noting in detail the evidence we have with respect to Paul's collection and presentation of his offering(s). Luke mentions two offerings Paul brought to Jerusalem. The first one mentioned was to alleviate the distress brought on by a worldwide famine:

> And the disciples determined, every one according to his ability, to send relief to the brethren who lived in Judea; and they did so, sending it to the elders by the hand of Barnabas and Saul

(Acts 11:29–30)

The reference to a second offering occurred during Paul's defense of himself before the Roman governor Felix against the accusations of Tertullus, the spokesman of the high priest Ananias and some other Jewish elders who had come from Jerusalem to press charges against Paul:

> Now after some years I came to bring to my nation alms and offerings. As I was doing this, they found me purified in the temple, without any crowd or tumult.

(Acts 24:17–18)

Although Paul's reference to his arrest later in the same speech is a clear allusion to his arrest after a disturbance in the temple, an arrest reported in Acts 21:27–36, there is no reference in that passage in Acts 21 to an offering as the reason for Paul's final journey to Jerusalem. Nor is there any hint there about the fate of that offering at the hands of the Jerusalem authorities.

Paul, however, refers twice to the collection in general terms (i.e., in addition to those places where he is advising his churches about actually assembling the money). The first reference is in the account of the meeting at which he agreed to make the collection:

> Only they would have us remember the poor, which very thing I was eager to do.
>
> (Gal. 2:10)

The second general reference to it occurs in his letter to the Roman Christians, when he explains yet one more delay (he expects it to be the final one) in his visit to them:

> At present, however, I am going to Jerusalem with aid for the saints. For Macedonia and Achaia have been pleased to make some contribution to the poor among the saints at Jerusalem; they were pleased to do it, and indeed they are in debt to them, for if the Gentiles have come to share in their spiritual blessing, they ought also to be of service to them in material blessings. When therefore I have completed this, and have delivered to them what has been raised, I shall go on by way of you to Spain. . . .
>
> (Rom. 15:25–28)

There is no evidence in Paul's letters to lead us to think these references were to two different offerings brought at different times to Jerusalem. The most reasonable conclusion to draw is that both passages refer to the same offering and the same journey. We do not learn of its results from Paul.

Luke, however, does mention two such visits, even if he refers to the second only in passing. It is not clear why he does that. On the one hand, he may well have had two traditions related to an offering Paul brought to Jerusalem, one or both with only vague references to the time and occasion.[17] He will then have interpreted his traditions as referring to two separate visits, and located them in the way that seemed best to him. On the other hand, he may have deliberately wanted to place the offering visit to Jerusalem earlier on in Paul's career rather than at its end, for apologetic reasons.[18] In either case, the double reference Luke makes to such a visit (Acts 11 and Acts 24) surely complicates the picture and makes it difficult to identify the report in Acts 11 with Paul's intended visit mentioned in Romans 15, as some have attempted to do.[19]

It is difficult to determine why Luke structured his accounts as he did. Perhaps he simply chose to ignore, in his account of Paul's last visit to Jerusalem (Acts 21:17—23:30, esp. 21:17–26), the information that Paul had at that time brought an offering, even though it seems apparent from Acts 24:17–18 that he did have a tradition to that effect. Or perhaps the tradition he had that reported (or that he interpreted as reporting) an earlier visit to Jerusalem with an offering seemed more important to him. In any case, because Luke thought the problem of Gentile-Jewish relations, and hence of unity in the church, had been resolved by the Apostolic Council and the Apostolic Decree reported in Acts 15, a visit by Paul to Jerusalem at the close of his career with an offering which was to seal (or even confirm) such a unity would have seemed highly inappropriate.[20]

5

THE SHAPE OF ACTS

We have now concluded our survey of the kind of traditions that Luke apparently possessed as he undertook to compose his narrative (Acts) of the course of the early church in its formative years. We have seen, further, that some of the information contained in those traditions is also reflected in the information Paul gives us in the first two chapters of his letter to the Galatian Christians when he recites his contacts with the religious authorities in Jerusalem.

The problem we face now is this: given the kind of traditions Luke had, and the sort of information they apparently contained, how can we account for the present shape of the narrative in Acts? The problem is given particular cogency precisely by those traditions that coincided with the information Paul presents in Galatians. One such tradition concerns the fact that Paul was not present at the meeting when the Apostolic Decree was formulated (no mention of it in Galatians 2; Acts 21:25 also assumes his absence). A second is the fact that his final trip to Jerusalem was prompted by Paul's desire to bring an offering to the Christians there (Rom. 15:25; Acts 24:17 also refers to it). In both cases, Luke ignored that evidence in favor of other information that he used in his narrative (in the case of the first, Acts 15; in the case of the second, perhaps Acts 11). How are we to account for the apparent discrepancies in Luke's own traditions, and for the choices he obviously made about which evidence he would use, and how he would use it?

That Luke was rather conservative in his use of traditions is shown by the very fact that he did include those pieces of information just mentioned which did not comport with the narrative he was constructing about the early church. Yet his use of sources in his Gospel also makes clear that he was quite capable of altering, omitting, and reinterpreting that information and those traditions. How then are we to account for the present shape of Acts?[1]

LUKE'S ASSUMPTIONS

To answer this question, we must examine the evidence Luke apparently had, as it comports with Paul's narrative in Galatians 1—2, in the light of certain assumptions Luke brought to his historical writing, and to the way he applied these assumptions in certain specific cases. What those tendencies were—the conviction that Christianity represented the legitimate outgrowth of Judaism, that the church underwent spectacular yet orderly growth under the direction of the apostles in Jerusalem, that harmony prevailed in the course of that development which was directed by the Holy Spirit—has often enough been discussed by commentators on Acts and they need not be rehearsed in detail here.[2] Given Luke's general view that the early church developed in internal harmony and external political innocuousness by divine direction under the authority of the Twelve in Jerusalem, I want to contend that Luke would have viewed the traditions he had, and the information they contained, in the following ways.

1. Luke would have assumed that an event in the life of the early church as important as the proclamation of the gospel to the Gentiles would surely have begun with one of the Twelve! However important he may have thought the role played by Paul in the missionary activity among the Gentiles to have been, and however important his traditions may have indicated Antioch as the origin of that mission to have been, it would not be at all surprising for Luke to have held such a conviction. For that reason, it would seem, Luke has identified the account of Peter and the conversion of the Gentile Cornelius (chap. 10) as the point where the gentile mission began. He has done so despite his own evidence to the contrary, namely, that the gentile mission was in fact begun by Jewish converts at Antioch:

> Now those who were scattered because of the persecution that arose over Stephen traveled as far as Phoenicia and Cyprus and Antioch, speaking the word to none except Jews. But there were some of them, men of Cyprus and Cyrene, who on coming to Antioch spoke to the Greeks also, preaching the Lord Jesus. And the hand of the Lord was with them, and a great number that believed turned to the Lord.
>
> (Acts 11:19–21)

That the origin of the gentile mission described here was not to be attributed to one of the Twelve is made the more certain by Luke's earlier statement in 8:2 that those thus scattered did in fact not include "the apostles," that is, the Twelve.

Despite those traditions to the contrary, however (traditions that included Paul's identification of Peter as the head of the mission to the Jews: Gal. 2:7b–8a), Luke, because of his conviction that all important events in the early church occurred under the direct guidance and supervision of the Twelve, simply assumed that the first gentile conversion occurred as a result of the activity of one of the Twelve, in this case Peter, rather than the activity of others who were not included in that group. He therefore shaped his narrative accordingly. That kind of conviction about the first gentile conversion would also mean that for Luke the first confrontation about such conversion would have to have occurred with one of the Twelve, rather than with one of those scattered at the time of the persecution of Stephen. Accordingly, Luke has shaped his narrative so that the confrontation does occur with Peter (Acts 11:1–18), once more despite Luke's own evidence to the contrary that such a dispute erupted at Antioch, not Jerusalem (Acts 15:1). The upshot of the first confrontation about the gentile mission, naturally enough, given its initiation by one of the Twelve, was the acknowledgment of its legitimacy (Acts 11:18).

2. Luke is very likely to have assumed that at any conference where major decisions were made (such as the resolution of the Jewish/gentile Christian problem), all the major actors would have been present. Not only will the Twelve, or surely their key representatives, have been present, but, given the nature of the problem (that is, the gentile mission), Luke will have assumed that other major figures in the controversy who represented the gentile mission will also have been present. That is to say, given Luke's assumption of the harmony that prevailed in the early church, he would not have conceived that so important a problem could have been solved in the absence of key participants from both sides.[3]

3. In addition to Luke's assumption, made clear from the way he formulated Acts 15 (see Appendix 2), that a conference to decide so important an issue for the primitive church must have included the ruling gremium in Jerusalem (i.e., "the apostles and the elders"), he apparently made some other assumptions from the information he had about that assembly. For example, he concluded that the information he had about a participant in that council named "Symeon" who

apparently took a leading role (Acts 15:7–11), was in fact information about "Simon" (i.e., Peter).[4] Luke could hardly have imagined that such a conference would have been held, and such important decisions reached (the Apostolic Decree), without the presence and active involvement of the very apostle with whom, in his view, the gentile mission began, namely, Peter (cf. Acts 15:7, 14).

Nor would Luke have been able to imagine that such deliberations about gentile Christians would have been undertaken without the presence and active participation of those who had become the leading figures in that mission, namely, Barnabas and Paul, as well as others from Antioch (Acts 15:2), the present center of that mission in Luke's view (and its likely place of origin; Acts 11:19–21). Accordingly, Paul and Barnabas are described by Luke as having given a report on their mission to the council (Acts 15:12).

Finally, since the result of the conference, the Apostolic Decree, had to be communicated to the gentile mission, Luke would naturally have assumed that the task of communicating it would have been entrusted to the key figures in that mission (Barnabas and Paul). Luke was also aware, however, that others were included in the party charged with that responsibility (Judas and Silas, 15:32).[5]

Apostolic Decree a Compromise

The Apostolic Decree, in Luke's view, must also have represented a compromise acceptable to all participants. There were concessions made by Jewish Christians: gentile converts were not to be burdened with the whole law, but needed only to observe some minimal requirements (Acts 15:19). Similarly, there were concessions made by gentile Christians: gentile converts would abandon the claim to be wholly free of the law and would in fact agree to submit to those minimal requirements. Let us see how Luke worked that out in detail.

COMPROMISE ACCEPTABLE TO PAUL

On the one hand, the compromise contained in the decree would have been acceptable to Paul, who, in Luke's understanding and presentation, remained a loyal Jew:

Do therefore what we [James and the elders in Jerusalem] tell you [Paul]. We have four men who are under a vow; take these man and purify yourself along with them and pay their expenses, so that they may shave their heads. Thus all will know that there is nothing in what they have been

39

told about you, but that you yourself live in observance of the law. . . .
Then Paul took the men, and the next day he purified himself with them
and went into the temple, to give notice when the days of purification
would be fulfilled and the offering presented for every one of them.

(Acts 21:23–24, 26)

[Paul to Felix] As you may ascertain, it is not more than twelve days since
I went up to worship at Jerusalem. . . . But this I admit to you, that according to the Way, which they call a sect, I worship the God of our fathers, believing everything laid down by the law or written in the prophets, having a hope in God which these themselves [the Jews who accused
Paul] accept, that there will be a resurrection of both the just and the un-
just. So I always take pains to have a clear conscience toward God and toward men.

(Acts 24:11, 14–16)

Paul said in his defense [to Festus], "Neither against the law of the Jews,
nor against the temple, nor against Caesar have I offended at all."

(Acts 25:8)

They [the Jews who accuse Paul] have known for a long time, if they are
willing to testify, that according to the strictest party of our religion I
have lived as a Pharisee. And now I stand here on trial for hope in the
promise made by God to our fathers, to which our twelve tribes hope to
attain, as they earnestly worship night and day. And for this hope I am
accused by Jews, O King [Agrippa]!

(Acts 26:5–7)

Therefore, when Paul was accused of being disloyal to the religion of
his fathers, the accusations were false:

And they [law-zealous Jews] have been told about you that you teach all
the Jews who are among the Gentiles to forsake Moses, telling them not
to circumcise their children or observe the customs. . . . [Jews from Asia
were] crying out, "Men of Israel, help! This is the man who is teaching
men everywhere against the people and the law and this place; moreover
he has brought Greeks into the temple, and he has defiled this holy
place."

(Acts 21:21, 28)

And they [Jews who accuse Paul before Felix] did not find me disputing
with any one or stirring up a crowd, either in the temple or in the synagogues, or in the city. Neither can they prove to you what they now
bring up against me.

(Acts 24:12–13)

COMPROMISE ACCEPTABLE TO JEWISH CHRISTIANS

On the other hand, the compromise contained in the decree would have been acceptable to the Jewish Christians, since in Luke's view they willingly listened to Peter when he pointed out the folly of requiring of Gentiles something Jews themselves had not been able to accomplish (Acts 15:10). They also willingly listened to James when he apparently advised against requiring circumcision of Gentiles ("Therefore my judgment is that we should not *trouble* those of the Gentiles who turn to God," 15:19, emphasis mine) because Amos had predicted, according to the Greek translation of the Old Testament (LXX), that "the rest of men" (i.e., Gentiles) would seek the Lord and be called by his name (apparently implying they had not become proselytes but remained Gentiles; 15:17–18). The upshot of the conference was that the Jerusalem church, and hence its Jewish-Christian wing, disavowed any attempt to require circumcision (15:24).

As a result of the Apostolic Decree, therefore, a compromise had been reached which those Christians zealous for the law could continue to find acceptable, and use as a basis for fellowship with gentile Christians.[6]

Therefore, in Luke's view, the problem of fellowship between Jewish and gentile Christians was resolved, and no real animosity between them can have remained. The church continued, in this as always, to be guided by the Holy Spirit (cf. 15:28).[7] That is probably why Luke has omitted any reference to circumcision or problems relating to it after Acts 15:1–5; he evidently assumed that it was dropped by common agreement, especially in light of Peter's speech (esp. vv. 9–11).[8]

4. In the light of the assumptions which Luke brought to his traditions about the early Christian community, it becomes clear why Luke concluded that the split in the gentile-Christian movement had to result from something other than the decision about the decree reached at the council.[9] Luke had a tradition that reported the dispute between Paul and Barnabas and their subsequent separation, but it may not have been clear on the reason for those events. Luke would not have been inclined to suppose that the separation could have been over so substantive an issue as Paul reports in Gal 2:11–14. That would have been to admit disruptive conflicts between Jewish and gentile Christians after they had settled their differences at the Apos-

41

tolic Council. Luke, needing a less disruptive motivation for the separation of Paul and Barnabas, found it in the story about the argument between them over whether John Mark should again accompany them on a missionary journey. By providing such a motivation, Luke makes the reason for the dispute and ensuing separation a matter of personalities rather than of substance, and the outcome of the dispute was a doubling rather than a curtailing of the mission to the Gentiles![10]

5. Because in Luke's view the Jerusalem conference settled in principle the issue of gentile-Jewish Christian relationships, he concluded that despite a report he had of an offering brought by Paul to Jerusalem from the gentile churches at the time of his arrest, that offering could not have come at the end of Paul's missionary career. As a result, Luke made nothing of the tradition he had (Acts 24:17–18) that the offering was in some way related to Paul's last visit to Jerusalem and his arrest there. Nor, in Luke's view, could the offering at the time of Paul's final visit have been associated with any attempt to establish unity between the two branches of the Christian community. The issue of unity had been settled long before that final journey to Jerusalem. Luke would therefore have been disinclined to think that unity would have figured either in that visit or in any offering Paul might have brought.

In the same way, Luke would not have thought such an offering, if Paul did bring it, would have been refused (cf. Rom. 15:31b). If it had been brought, it would surely have been gratefully received, and, in the absence of any such information, Luke ignored the tradition of the later offering. Rather, despite the evidence he had to the contrary, reflected in Acts 24:17–18, Luke located the offering journey much earlier in Paul's career (Acts 11:27–30) and gave it a motivation other than the display of unity it was intended to have according to Paul's own report of it (Gal. 2:10; cf. Rom. 15:25–27).[11]

SUMMARY

We have, then, two accounts (Acts and Galatians) of the ongoing relationship between the gentile mission in general and Paul in particular, on the one side, and the Christian authorities in Jerusalem, on the other. Yet those two accounts differ from each other. We are therefore inevitably faced with the question about what the actual course of events may have been that gave rise to the two differing reports. We have already seen that Luke's understanding of the way the early church must have developed has affected the way he interpreted the traditions he had, and hence influenced the way he presented his account of that development in Acts.[12] We have also seen that although the way Paul has described some of those same events differs from the way Luke presented them, Luke nevertheless apparently had evidence that in some instances supported Paul's reports in Galatians 1—2 precisely where they differed from the narrative in Acts.[13]

Can we, taking into account the characteristics of the two narratives and the traditions they contain, come to any supportable conclusions about the events that underlie those narratives of Paul's relationship with the Jerusalem authorities and of his journeys to that city to visit and confer, perhaps even dispute, with them? I believe we can, and it is to the task of outlining those events as they can be recovered that we must now turn.

6

THE EVENTS UNDERLYING ACTS AND GALATIANS

We must now turn our attention to the attempt to outline the events about which both Paul and Luke report, in light of the rather different way those two accounts are shaped. Again, we will limit ourselves to those events that concern Paul's relationship with the Christian authorities in Jerusalem, events recited by Paul principally in Galatians 1—2, and by Luke in Acts 11—15, with other references scattered throughout that narrative.

PAULINE PRIORITY

In light of our argument for the priority of the Pauline narrative over the material in Acts, we want to urge now that priority in this reconstruction of events must not be given to the two visits of Paul to Jerusalem that are recorded in Acts: the famine visit (Acts 11:27–30) and the visit for the Apostolic Council (Acts 15:1–29).[1] Rather, contrary to the usual procedure for those who attempt to reconstruct these events, we shall give priority to the two visits to Jerusalem that Paul records in Galatians: the visit to see Peter (Gal. 1:18–24), and the amicable solution of the problem of gentile-Jewish Christian relationships (Gal. 2:1–10). Such a setting of priorities means that instead of assuming for our reconstruction the reliability of the general order and content of Paul's visits to Jerusalem reported in Acts, and fitting the visits reported in Galatians into that framework, we shall begin with the accounts of the visits recorded in Galatians. Assuming the general reliability of their order and content, we shall then see what events, reported in Acts, appear to be consonant with Paul's account in Galatians.

44

That one ought to give priority to the account in Galatians over the account in Acts has of course been acknowledged by many scholars for a number of years. Yet it would appear that its implications for understanding the course of the events of the early church, events reflected in the two accounts we have in Galatians and Acts, have not been presented in such a way as to take that insight systematically into account. If in fact the material in Paul, as John Knox and others long ago argued, is to be accorded priority, then that priority ought to include not only the content and order of events reported, but ought also to be made the point from which an investigation of those events is to begin. It is precisely the point of departure, normally taken from the narratives in Acts, that has allowed Acts to continue to exert undue influence on the historical reconstructions of the underlying events, even on those reconstructions undertaken by scholars who acknowledge the need to accord priority to the Pauline material. Sufficient attention has all too infrequently been given to this point, which has then had its effects on the results obtained. Priority in the following discussion will therefore fall to the material recorded by Paul (especially Galatians), and our starting point will be the order in which he reports his visits to Jerusalem, and the relationship he had with the authorities resident there and with their authority as it reached beyond the boundaries of that city.

A second point about methodological priority also needs to be made. Given the presuppositions—the biases, if one will—which are operative in the narratives in Acts, it is advisable to give higher value to the evidence that stands independent of those presuppositions, rather than to the evidence that supports them. That is simply because at those places in the narrative in Acts where Luke's presuppositions are most in evidence, one cannot be sure whether they represent the underlying events or whether Luke has shaped inadequate or fragmentary accounts in light of his presuppositions. It is therefore precisely at those places in Acts where the biases are most in evidence that one must suspect a distortion of the underlying events. Conversely, at those points where a tradition appears in Acts in a context where it does not serve a presupposition common to the narrative in Acts, that tradition may be accorded greater probative value, simply because it shows no signs of having been accommodated to Luke's presuppositions. In other words, at those points where a tradition appears in Acts in a context where it does not reflect a presupposition common to the narrative in Acts, that tradition should be given priority as evidence over a tradition occurring in a context clearly favorable to a Lukan presupposition.

One further point needs to be made concerning methodological priority and the material in Acts. Where there is a tradition that does not support a Lukan presupposition and where, in addition, that tradition agrees with, or at least is neutral over against, a similar tradition in Paul, that tradition must be given great weight in our reconstruction.[2] This is simply because in such a case we have two independent witnesses to a given event, Paul and Luke, and hence we may have greater confidence that in those cases we are on the track of historical actuality.

Examples

Examples will help to clarify the point here being made. As a first example, we may consider Luke's account of Paul's offering which he brought to Jerusalem. Acts contains a reference to the offering being brought to Jerusalem at the time of Paul's final visit there, a point Luke makes only in passing (Acts 24:17). The other reference to an offering being brought to Jerusalem by Paul occurs in Acts 11 in relation to a purported worldwide famine at a much earlier time. That account, which is placed much earlier in the narrative (Acts 11:27–30), allowed Luke to avoid the negative implications for church unity which would have been embodied in a rejection of the offering. Yet that rejection is hinted at in Acts (24:18–19), and it is something Paul clearly anticipated as a possibility (Rom. 15:31). In this case, therefore, priority would be given the tradition that located Paul's gift at the time of his last visit to Jerusalem, something on which Paul and Acts agree. In addition, that understanding of events stands in contradiction to a fuller account about the offering in Acts, an account that clearly served Luke's purpose of emphasizing the harmony in the early church. That is, by placing the offering earlier and motivating it by famine, not unity, Luke avoided mention of a conflict between Paul and the Jerusalem Christians at the end of Paul's missionary career.[3]

As a second example, we may consider the traditions about Paul and the Apostolic Decree. Acts contains a passing reference to the decree when James reports to Paul James's action in sending to the gentile Christians a letter containing the list of the exhortations contained in the decree. James there clearly assumes he is informing Paul of something about which Paul would know nothing! Acts also contains an account of the Apostolic Decree, however, according to which

Paul was both present when it was formulated, and was also one of the bearers of the letter itself (Acts 15:1–27). This latter account allows Luke to make clear that something so important for the gentile mission as the Apostolic Decree must have involved Paul not only in its formulation but also in its dissemination. That in its turn allows Luke to present the Decree as representing a compromise fully acceptable both to Jewish and gentile Christian leaders. Again, there is little clear evidence in Paul's letters that he was aware of any such council at which the Apostolic Decree was formulated (see Gal. 2:10), or for that matter that he was ever aware of the content of the decree.

Once again, a tradition Luke mentions in passing—in this instance, that Paul was informed of the decree at a point subsequent to its formulation and dissemination—stands in general agreement with Paul's account and is to be preferred to Luke's fuller account. It is to be preferred not only because it agrees with Paul but also because the fuller account allows Luke to present a picture of the unity of the early church at work, a point fully in accord with his assumptions about the course of development in the early church.

In summary, we propose to use a method in the following discussion which gives priority to the Pauline order of the visits to Jerusalem reported in Galatians over the order of those visits reported in Acts. We will therefore seek to fit accounts in Acts into the Pauline framework rather than the reverse. Furthermore, we will give preference to the evidence in Acts which operates outside the bounds of Luke's presuppositions, or even contrary to them, rather than to other references to the same or similar events in Acts which clearly fit Luke's overall purposes in the composing of his narratives. In those cases where the preferred traditions in Acts also stand in accord with Paul's account of the same or similar events, we will assume that we are closer to accounts of the actual events than in any other instance. Using these criteria, we must now examine in more detail the records we have.

MEETINGS IN JERUSALEM

Gal. 1:18–21. The visit with which we must start our investigation is therefore the first one mentioned by Paul (Gal. 1:18–21). Which visit in Acts most clearly fits our criteria of more reliable evidence? While many have argued that the first visit Paul made to Jerusalem as reported in Galatians 1 is to be construed as parallel to the "famine visit" recorded in Acts 11:27–30, it would seem more appropriate to find its parallel in the first visit of Paul to Jerusalem as recorded in

Acts: the visit recorded in Acts 9:26. Here Paul's claim that on his first
visit to Jerusalem he did not see all the Twelve, emphasized under
oath, is reflected in Acts' language that on that first visit the disciples
did not want to see him, doubting the sincerity of his conversion:

> And when he had come to Jerusalem he attempted to join the disciples;
> and they were all afraid of him, for they did not believe that he was a dis-
> ciple. But Barnabas took him, and brought him to the apostles, and de-
> clared to them how on the road he had seen the Lord, who spoke to him,
> and how at Damascus he had preached boldly in the name of Jesus.
>
> (Acts 9:26–27)

We note that the latter part of the story contains the account of Barnabas, one who had an earlier relation to the Twelve, introducing Paul
to the Twelve, and telling them about Paul's conversion and Paul's
subsequent preaching in Damascus. This latter part of the story brings
the whole tradition into line with Luke's presupposition about the
Twelve (Paul would have to meet all the leaders in Jerusalem before he
could begin his mission in earnest). It also brings the tradition into accord with his earlier account of Paul's conversion, where the meaning
of the conversion itself had to be explained and its significance confirmed by someone already a member of the Christian community
(Acts 9:10–22).[4]

Apart from those elements which reflect Luke's interests, however,
we have in Acts an account of Paul's first visit to Jerusalem as a Christian apostle which does in fact bear a positive relationship to Paul's
own account of his first visit there.

Gal. 2:1–10. The next visit to Jerusalem that Paul reports is found
in Gal. 2:1–10. At that visit, the problems of the relationship between
the Jewish and gentile Christian missions found their amicable solution. This visit has its clearest echo, not in Acts 15:1–29, so often
cited, or even in Acts 11:27–30,[5] but rather in Acts 11:1–18!

We noted earlier that Luke, with his conviction that an undertaking
as important as the mission to the Gentiles must have originated with
one of the Twelve, has located that origin with Peter (Acts 10:1–48;
cf. 15:7) rather than with some Jewish Christians in Antioch, despite
the tradition he had to that effect (Acts 11:19–21). Paul of course be-
trays no knowledge of any tradition that the gentile mission was begun by Peter. In Paul's report, Peter was associated with the mission

to the Jews, not to the Gentiles (Gal. 2:7: "Peter had been entrusted with the gospel to the circumcised").

Further, because Luke regarded Peter as the first to open the gentile mission, he then assumed, logically enough, that the questions to which that mission gave rise would first have been faced by the originator of it—Peter himself. It is for that reason, I want to contend, that Luke has omitted mention of Paul in his first account of a confrontation on the problem posed for Jewish-Christian authorities by the admission of Gentiles to the Christian community apart from the requirement that they be circumcised. That confrontation, as Luke reports it, did result in an amicable solution.

The following table will summarize the correlation for which I am arguing:

Gal. 1:18–21 // Acts 9:26
Gal. 2:1–10 // Acts 11:1–18

Many scholars have of course argued that Paul's second trip to Jerusalem narrated in Gal. 2:1–10 is to be paralleled to the account of the Apostolic Council in Jerusalem reported in Acts 15:1–29. Careful examination will show, however, that although a number of the details in Gal. 2:1–10 do not comport well with the account in Acts 15:1–29, they do betray a similarity to the details contained in the account in Acts 11:1–18. For example, the issue in Acts 11:3 is the association of Jews with those who were uncircumcised, with the implicit demand that all who would become Christians must be circumcised. It is that very situation that is reflected in Paul's remark about the apparent pressure upon him to have Titus circumcised. The fact that Titus did not have to be circumcised (Gal. 2:3)[6] corresponds to the outcome reflected in Acts 11:18.

It also reflects the outcome of the meeting recorded in Acts 15:1–29, to be sure, but the resolution there did not in the end concern itself with circumcision, despite the fact that circumcision was the original question (Acts 15:1, 5). Rather, the resolution there was framed in terms of the Apostolic Decree, with no mention of circumcision at all. The clear implication of the outcome of the conference reported in Acts 11:18, on the other hand, is that no circumcision be required of Gentiles, since to them "also God has granted repentance unto life," that is, salvation, even without circumcision.

Again, while James played a role (he is named first in Gal. 2:9 in most manuscripts),[7] there is no compelling evidence in the Pauline account in Galatians 2 that he had by that time taken over leadership of the Jerusalem church from Peter.[8] Indeed, Peter was the key Jerusalem participant, and played a more prominent role in the meeting as Paul described it (e.g., Gal. 2:7–8), a situation more closely reflected in Acts 11:1–18 than in Acts 15:1–29. (It may well have been information about Peter's key role in Luke's otherwise sparse and fragmentary traditions concerning the events reported in Acts 11:1–18 that led him to conclude that the conference involved Peter alone.) By limiting the first conference to Peter, Luke could allow both for James to assume prominence and for the second conference to be resolved with the Apostolic Decree, points he seemed to deem important to make.

Finally, the nature of the assembly described in Acts 11:1–18 is quite informal, much more so than the more formal Apostolic Council as reported by Luke in Acts 15. In that respect also the conference in Acts 11 conforms better to Paul's almost offhand remark that his conference with the three pillars was a private affair (Gal. 2:2). Such a remark would be totally out of keeping with the kind of conference Luke described as concluding with the Apostolic Decree (present were "apostles and elders," 15:1; "the brethren, both the apostles and the elders," 15:23; in addition, Peter, James, Barnabas, and Paul by name, 15:7, 12, 13).

Thus, Paul's account of the first conference about the gentile mission (Gal. 2:1–10; Barnabas's presence indicates that it did not concern Paul's mission exclusively),[9] ended in agreement that Gentiles did not have to take upon themselves the obligation of the law (implied by the [refused] requirement for circumcision, v. 3).[10] That same point is reflected in Luke's narrative in Acts 11:1–18. Again, that first conference in Jerusalem concerning the gentile mission which Luke reports in Acts 11 ended amicably, with an agreement[11] fully in accord with Paul's understanding of the gentile mission (Gal. 2:9; cf. Acts 11:18). That Luke would have omitted from this account any mention of an offering is apparent from the way he understood, or at least presented, that offering when he does discuss it (Acts 11:27–30): it was to aid hunger, not church unity (v. 29). Again, if the "comity arrangement" of Gal. 2:9 (Peter to Jews, Paul and Barnabas to Gentiles) is missing in the narrative in Acts 11:1–18, the approval of a gentile mission with no requirements to be laid upon converts is nevertheless clearly implied by the reaction of those who had demanded circumcision:

And when they heard this [Peter's account of the conversion of Cornelius] they were silenced. And they glorified God, saying, "Then to the Gentiles also God has granted repentance unto life."

(Acts 11:18)

On the basis of such a conclusion, one gets the impression that the question of circumcision for gentile converts to Christianity had finally been resolved. One gets the same impression from Paul's account in Gal. 2:1–10: the matter had now been laid to rest. Yet that was not the case. Luke was forced to portray an account where it did arise again (Acts 15:1, 5), and then yet again (see also 21:20–21, even after 15:23–29). Paul's further discussion in Galatians shows that it reappeared despite the settlement that is portrayed in Galatians 2:9–10 (see Gal. 5:2–6, 11–12; 6:12). All of that attests to the truly intractable nature of this problem.[12]

How long that agreement lasted is difficult to determine, but the confrontation between Paul, on the one side, and Peter and Barnabas, on the other, indicates that, whatever the nature of the agreement that had existed, it was at that point called decisively into question. Where Jewish and gentile Christians had been sharing table fellowship, news brought by "men from James" now caused the Jewish Christians to withdraw from, and thus end, such fellowship (Gal. 2:11–13). What therefore had been possible before "men from James" arrived was from that point on no longer possible. What had occurred to cause that change?

It was, we want to urge, precisely the council which Luke reports in Acts 15,[13] at which James, who had now assumed sole leadership in Jerusalem, presided (note that Peter was in Antioch, Gal. 2:11). It was at that conference that the decision was reached that minimal legal restrictions of a cultic nature had to be observed by gentile converts.[14] It is clear from Paul's account that apart from such observance on the part of the gentile Christians, their recognition by Jewish believers as full-fledged Christians, and so of course table fellowship between the two parties, was no longer possible. It was the willingness of Peter and Barnabas to credit that decree, and the unwillingness of Paul to do so, we contend, that precipitated the disagreement and split in the gentile mission in Antioch.[15]

HISTORICAL RECONSTRUCTION—A PROPOSAL

The events which underlie those accounts will have run their course in the following way: At some point after the agreement recorded in

Gal. 2:9–10 had been reached, or perhaps even because of it, Peter had left Jerusalem to embark on his mission to the Jews (Gal. 2:7b, 9c; on Peter's leaving Jerusalem prior to the Apostolic Conference, see Acts 12:17), and James had assumed primary leadership.[16] Subsequently, Jewish Christian dissatisfaction with the "private" decision reached between Paul and the three "pillar apostles" will have reached a point where it had to be dealt with. There is, as we noted above, evidence for the fact that the dispute concerning whether or not Gentiles needed to be circumcised, or obey at least part of the Jewish law, was a continuing one. It can be found in Acts 11:2; 15:1; 21:10–21; Gal. 2:11; 5:2–6, 11–12; 6:12; 1 Cor. 1:11–12; and perhaps a reflection of it is to be found in Rom. 2:28–29.[17]

As a result of such increasing dissatisfaction with the decision reached in private between Paul and the three apostles, we would argue that a further conference was held in Jerusalem, at which Antioch was represented by a delegation headed by Symeon Niger (Acts 15:14; cf. 13:1),[18] and perhaps also including Silas and Judas Barsabbas (Acts 15:22, 27, 32).[19] It was at this conference, at the insistence of the Jewish Christians whom Luke elsewhere identifies as the "circumcision party" (Acts 11:2; cf. 15:1, 5)—whether with the active assistance of James or not we cannot tell[20]—that the Apostolic Decree was formulated[21] and announced by personal emissaries (probably also by letter from James; see Acts 21:25) to the center of the gentile mission, notably Antioch. No doubt this was done under the assumption that it would be further disseminated from there (Acts 15:23, 27).

It was from these emissaries, sent by James who surely presided over this conference in Jerusalem, that Peter, Barnabas, and Paul learned of the conference and its decisions about legal requirements to be observed by gentile Christians if they were to be suitable for table fellowship with Jewish Christians (Gal. 2:12).[22] As Acts 21:25 confirms, the decisions did come from James, and it was in his name that they were communicated to the leaders of the gentile mission, including Paul and Barnabas.[23]

The willingness of Peter and Barnabas, along with the other Jewish Christians, to abide by those restrictions (Gal. 2:12b–13)—a willingness signaled by their withdrawal from table fellowship[24] with those who, perhaps under the direct influence of Paul, did not— precipitated the split. It is clear, furthermore, that the split was not only between Jewish and gentile Christians but was also a split within the gentile mission itself ("even Barnabas," Gal. 2:13b).[25] It is this split which is reflected in the "sharp contention" about which Luke knew from his traditions, and mention of which he included in Acts 15:39, but for which he provided another motivation, one less explosive to the unity of the church.

While the events recited in Gal. 2:11–14 could have occurred shortly after the conference described in Gal. 2:1–10, there is no necessity for that to have been the case.[26] Paul of course gives no indication of the interval between Gal. 2:10 and 2:11. On the basis of his own narrative, however, one need not presume that the Antioch incident occurred immediately after the meeting described in 2:1–10. The interval between the events recited in 1:18 and 2:1 shows that long periods of time could elapse between the events Paul was reciting. The fact that Paul does not indicate a specific interval here may be due to the fact that he has now begun to focus his attention more directly on the problem that had arisen among the Galatian Christians. It was with that point that he was primarily concerned in his letter, and his mind may well have been on that problem rather than on a recitation of a chronology of the events leading up to this confrontation at Antioch.

The reaction of Peter, Barnabas, and (apparently) others to the news brought by the "men from James" was particularly upsetting for Paul, as his reaction indicates: "Cephas . . . stood condemned;" he "feared the circumcision party;" he with "the rest of the Jews acted hypocritically, so that even Barnabas was carried away by their hypocrisy" (Gal. 2:11–13). There was ample ground, from Paul's perspective, for such a reaction. Peter's willingness to adhere to the demands of the circumcision party, news of whose evident victory in Jerusalem was conveyed by the men James sent, abrogated the agreement Paul had thought he had reached not only with Peter, but also with James. Despite that "right hand of fellowship" which had sealed the agreement to allow the gentile mission to proceed undisturbed by any legal demands, first James, and then Peter (and even his coworker in the gentile mission, Barnabas!) had now by their acts gone back on their word. One suspects it was precisely this background that explains the outrage which underlay Paul's "correction" of Peter as a result of Peter's actions.[27]

In light of that earlier meeting between Paul and the three "pillar apostles" in Jerusalem, Paul could only understand this new turn of events—the imposition of the Apostolic Decree on gentile Christians by James and the acquiescent reaction by Peter demonstrated in his withdrawal from table fellowship with them—as a direct contradiction to that earlier solemn agreement. It was an act which in effect unilaterally abrogated it![28] One suspects therefore that feelings of personal betrayal as well as theological disagreement lie behind Paul's outburst against Peter recorded in Gal. 2:11.[29]

It is quite possible, on the other hand, that James and the other authorities in Jerusalem, as well as the representatives of gentile Christianity from Antioch (among others, Symeon Niger, as we have suggested), had hoped that Paul would agree to the decree, since it did not require circumcision, the issue at the earlier Jerusalem conference Paul had attended (Gal. 2:3–5).[30] Given Paul's demonstrated advice to conform one's behavior to the needs of others (e.g., 1 Cor. 8:7–13; 10:23–32; Rom. 14:1—15:6), and his own willingness to "become as one under the law" to further his missionary enterprise (1 Cor. 9:20), his refusal could have been equally surprising to the participants in the Jerusalem Council that formulated the decree. Perhaps it was more the unilateral reversal of the earlier agreement, and Paul's correct fear that even this would not satisfy the Jewish Christians, that lay behind Paul's abrupt rejection of the decree.

THE CAUSES FOR DISAGREEMENT

What had happened in Jerusalem or elsewhere to cause James to change his stance from the earlier agreement cited by Paul in Gal. 2:9 to the decision the news of which caused the confrontation in Antioch, we can only guess. Perhaps a more radical Jewish-Christian group gained the ascendancy in Jerusalem, and forced the decision on James. Perhaps, on the other hand, James's earlier acceptance of the agreement struck between Paul and himself as one of the three "pillar apostles" had been reluctant. Now, having assumed the leadership in Jerusalem, he was free to shape decisions more in line with his own convictions. Perhaps, as a third possibility, external conditions had changed, so that what had been acceptable to the Jerusalem authorities at an earlier time was so no longer.[31] Whatever pressures there may have been on the Christian community, however, whether internal or external, it is evident that as Paul understood it, a major shift had taken place in the attitude of James and the Jerusalem authorities. It was a shift that Paul felt he could not tolerate.

Paul's dissatisfaction with the decision of that Jerusalem conference that gentile Christians must observe minimal legal restrictions, and hence his opposition to them, continued throughout the time of his mission about which we know through his letters. That opposition was probably based on his conviction that to observe them meant "part Christ, part law," a position he found impossible. He had argued specifically against that position in Galatians, in a situation which by his own telling was directly relevant to this problem (Gal. 2:18; cf. Rom. 7:4, 6). The reason for Paul's opposition was his conviction that the law could add nothing to the grace of Christ which was received in faith (Gal. 2:21). Indeed, the law itself was fulfilled in such faith (Gal. 5:13–14; cf. Rom. 10:4). Any attempt to return to the law thus meant to turn away from grace (to be "severed from Christ;" Gal 5:4).[32]

From all appearances the Jewish Christians who had their center in Jerusalem were also dissatisfied with the "solution" to the gentile-Jewish Christian problem represented in the Apostolic Decree. Even after its promulgation, they continued to proclaim that unless one were circumcised (and hence became a Jew) one could not truly be a Christian (cf. Gal. 5:2–3, 11–12; 6:12—verses that were obviously written after the Jerusalem conference that had formulated the decree, and against which Paul had reacted in Antioch).[33] Thus, instead of solving the problem of unity within the body of believers, as Luke portrayed the events,[34] the Jerusalem conference and its decree succeeded only in splitting the gentile mission without in any way mollifying the radical Jewish Christians. Their opposition, as Luke himself knew (cf. Acts 21:20b–24), continued to the end of Paul's ministry.

7

SOME HISTORICAL
CONCLUSIONS

We have now reviewed the evidence and suggested a course of events that would account for the shape of the reports of those events we now have in Acts and Galatians, events relating to Paul's contact with the church authorities in Jerusalem, and the kinds of arrangements that prevailed, and did not prevail, between them. What conclusions can now be drawn about this historical situation which produced the accounts we now have from Luke and Paul?

The conclusions we draw will depend in large measure on the understanding we have of the relationship of the Apostolic Decree (Acts 15:20, 29; 21:25) to the dispute in Antioch between Peter and Paul, caused by the arrival of men sent by James who brought news that split the church (Gal. 2:11–13). It is to that understanding that we must now return.

CONFLICT RESOLVED

There appears to be a general consensus among those who seek to find the outline and order of the events that underlie our two reports in Acts and Galatians that the Jerusalem Council reported in Acts 15 was probably the *result* of the kind of conflict between Jewish and gentile Christians that we find reported in Gal. 2:11–13.[1] On the basis of that view, the course of events can then be understood to have unfolded in the following way: During the initial period of the gentile mission, with its startlingly successful results, there had been no time to attempt to coordinate that mission with the kind of Christianity that was prevalent in the early church in and around Jerusalem. That understanding of the Christian faith saw itself as an outgrowth of Judaism, and, indeed, found its legitimacy in that fact, a legitimacy guaranteed by circumcision and observance of the law.

In those circumstances, however, it was only a matter of time before the law-free gospel of the gentile mission and the legal framework of Jewish Christianity came into conflict with one another. Although the problem of circumcision had been resolved, so this view continues (cf. Acts 11:2, 18; 15:1, 10), the problem about the validity of other matters of the law had not, and it was a dispute about them that caused a breach within the church. That dispute came to a head, as one might expect, in Antioch, the origin and center of the gentile mission. That is the conflict portrayed in Gal. 2:11–13.

It was in response to that conflict, this view further holds, that the council in Jerusalem was convened. At this council the possibility of future conflicts of such a kind was resolved through the reaffirmation of the freedom of gentile Christians from circumcision, and by applying to them those requirements which Leviticus 17—18 had applied to the non-Hebrews living in the midst of the Hebrew people. Thus the question of Jewish-gentile Christian fellowship was resolved, harmony was restored to the church,[2] and Paul was free to continue his mission in good conscience, secure in the knowledge that he was free from any future harassment by those who would require all Christians to become Jews.[3] It was, after all, as Luke reported it in Acts (15:1–2), just such a problem that had occurred in Antioch before the Jerusalem Council. It had been the impetus for holding that Council and for reaching the solution Luke represented as the Apostolic Decree. In this view, if the Corinthian correspondence occurred earlier than the conference that produced the decree, and shows no knowledge of it, it does show that Paul would have been open to that kind of compromise. If this correspondence was written after the conference, it may well show how Paul applied the decree in his continuing mission.[4]

On the basis of that kind of reconstruction of the order of events underlying the accounts in Acts 15 and Galatians 2, one can then conclude that the remainder of Paul's mission in the eastern Mediterranean world was carried, at least in Paul's view, to a successful conclusion (so Rom. 15:23).[5] In fact, on this view, but for his arrest in Jerusalem, Paul's plan to continue his missionary enterprise in the western half of that world (so Rom. 15:28) would have taken place. In that eventuality, Paul would have crowned one success with another.[6] Thus, this view concludes, if Acts errs in chronological detail, nevertheless it was at least correct in portraying the successful resolution of the relationship between the leaders of the Jerusalem church and Paul. The final upshot of these events, therefore, is that unity was preserved in that early period of the development of the church.[7]

CONFLICT UNRESOLVED

There is, however, as we saw in the last chapter, another way to construe the events recorded in Acts and their relationship to what Paul reports in Galatians 2. If the Apostolic Decree is understood not as the *result* of the conflict in Antioch reported in Gal. 2:11–14, but as the *cause* of that conflict, then a very different interpretation must be put on the ensuing course of events. It will force us to interpret the evidence concerning the events subsequent to the dispute in Antioch, evidence found both in Acts and in Paul, in a way other than Luke, and most scholars, have done. That "Lukan" way has been to see those events as resulting in the restoration of unity in the church, an interpretation that is clearly implied if the Jerusalem conference of Acts 15 (Apostolic Council) was called in *response* to the dispute in Antioch, and managed to resolve it. If, however, we follow the hint given in Luke, where the dispute between Paul and Barnabas that resulted in their separation (15:36–40) was *subsequent* to the Jerusalem Conference, then we must take seriously the fact that it was the *results* of the conference that caused the dispute in Antioch, not the dispute that caused the conference. In that case, there is no further conference to which we can appeal for a restoration of the unity fractured at Antioch. That way of interpreting the evidence has far-reaching consequences for our understanding of the subsequent development of the church, consequences quite different from those normally drawn. We must now turn to an examination of those consequences, to see what they imply about the course of events in the early church, particularly in relation to Paul and his mission.

The conclusion which forces itself upon us when we read Paul's account of his confrontation in Antioch with Peter "and the rest of the Jews," and finally also with Barnabas, is that Paul did not fare well in that confrontation. That would of course be true whether the Antioch dispute occurred prior to, or as the result of, the Jerusalem conference and the Apostolic Decree. But if the dispute was the *result* of the conference, then we cannot assume the dispute was resolved *at* that conference. We must instead reckon with an ongoing tension in the church, a tension at which Luke again hints when he reports no reconciliation between Paul and Barnabas. Luke's last reference to Barnabas in Acts is precisely in connection with his dispute with Paul, which Luke also locates in Antioch (Acts 15:39).

Paul, then, did not fare well in the encounter in Antioch. It is also rather clear that the dispute there was not resolved in his favor.[8] Had that been the case, Paul would surely have noted that fact, as he did with regard to the favorable results of his second visit to Jerusalem and the conference there with James, Peter, and John (Gal. 2:6b–10).[9] Rather, the church at Antioch supported not Paul but his opponents: Peter, Barnabas, and the men from James. In a word, Paul was the loser in that dispute! Not only the Jews but also Peter and Barnabas, a leading figure in the gentile mission, dramatized this reality when they observed the requirements of the Apostolic Decree, and as a result withdrew from table fellowship with those who did not observe them. The only one, apparently, who supported Paul was Silas (also called Silvanus; cf. Acts 15:49).[10] Silas then took the place of Barnabas as Paul's companion on his missionary travels (Luke also knew this: cf. Acts 16:19, 25, 29; 17:4, 10, 14–15; 18:5); he apparently had also accompanied Paul prior to Barnabas's separation from Paul (cf. 2 Cor. 1:19; 1 Thess. 1:1).

In a significant way, therefore, the dispute at Antioch was a watershed for the Pauline mission. Prior to that time, Paul had believed himself to be operating, as indeed he had every reason to believe, with the approval of the authorities in Jerusalem, and with the support of the Antioch community. After the dispute, however, he lost Antioch as his "power base,"[11] and, as Acts confirms, had to move further and further west to find room for his missionary activity.[12]

Yet even there, Paul was hounded by opponents,[13] people who may well have been the same sort of "men from James," with the same message that had precipitated the dispute at Antioch and had caused Paul to break not only with the Jerusalem church but also with some of those who up until that point had been his co-workers.[14] There is a hint in the language Paul uses in Gal. 2:6 that he did think the Jerusalem authorities were behind his difficulties. In that verse Paul refers to the "pillar apostles" and their high reputation in the past tense ("What they *were then* makes no difference to me"; emphasis mine) giving the clear impression that he no longer shares that evaluation.[15] It is this change in circumstances (Galatians was of course written after the confrontation in Antioch which is reported in this letter) rather than any reference to an earlier meeting that caused Paul to use the past tense in his reference to James, Peter, and John.[16] In

Paul's view, that earlier reputation had now become *adiaphora*, precisely because their subsequent activity had shown them to be anything but "pillars" of the church.

In Paul's view, however, one chance remained for him to restore the previous unity between himself and the Jerusalem authorities. That was the collection for the poor which had been agreed upon by both sides, and which had earlier resulted in the "right hand of fellowship" (Gal. 2:10) from precisely those pillars who had since, in Paul's view, broken that agreement. Thus Paul, hewing to that agreement, was determined that the collection be taken to Jerusalem. He apparently was motivated in that by the hope that such a gesture of his faithfulness to that agreement despite its being broken by others could yet restore the unity that had prevailed when that agreement was originally reached. There was a further point involved in that collection. It was the implied acknowledgment that the collection represented the indebtedness to the Jewish Christians on the part of the Gentiles for spiritual blessings (see Rom. 15:27; cf. 2 Cor. 8:13–14). That point may well have given Paul further hope that the gift might yet be accepted and the breach thereby healed.

Yet even here, as Paul had feared (despite his hope to the contrary: Rom. 15:30–31), he met with no success in this endeavor. From all indications, and we are limited here to Acts, his offering was not accepted and he was not delivered from "the unbelievers in Judea" (Rom. 15:31).[17] The silence of Acts about that last collection speaks volumes. Its rejection confirmed the lack of precisely that unity that Luke was so intent on portraying, and hence, though Luke knew about that offering (Acts 24:17), he chose not to report anything about it. Nor was Luke able to find any tradition of any support at all given to Paul by the Christians in Jerusalem after his arrest. Again, had any occurred, Luke would have hastened to mention it as further confirmation of the unity within the early church. The best Luke could do was report the nice welcome Paul received when he first arrived in Jerusalem (Acts 21:17; 20a); that and nothing more. Again, his silence on that score is eloquent.[18]

Our evidence therefore points to something other than the supposed final triumph of unity between Paul and Jerusalem which is found if the Apostolic Decree is seen as the result of the Antioch dispute. On the contrary, if, as the evidence seems to indicate, the Antioch dispute occurred *because* of the Jerusalem conference presided over by James, namely, the Apostolic Council that formulated and promulgated the Apostolic Decree, then we must acknowledge that unity was not restored in the end. Indeed, the tension between Jewish and gentile Christians which had been present from the beginning of the Christian mission as reported in Acts never was resolved.

THE PAULINE MISSION

This reconstruction requires a totally different understanding of the results of Paul's missionary endeavors. While one cannot and ought not doubt his effectiveness as a missionary to the Gentiles, one must acknowledge that his mission was never free from harassment by those who disputed his understanding of the gospel of Jesus Christ, something amply borne out in his own letters. Paul, it seems very likely, ended his career an isolated figure,[19] whose theological emphases were destined for swift decline in the decades to follow. Perhaps his desire to go to Spain because he no longer had "any room for work in these regions" (Rom. 15:23a) is not to be understood in the mood of hope, as the happy statement of a triumphant missionary who had completed part of his task and now looked forward to similar success in the other, western half of the Mediterranean world. Perhaps instead it must be understood as a sorrowful confession of defeat,[20] spoken in the hope that in Spain he might finally outrun his opponents and find surcease from Christian opposition to his proclamation of the gospel.

That is not a pleasant picture, and it stands at odds with the way these events are normally understood to have run, particularly among Protestant scholars for whom Paul is the hero of the faith. That picture of a triumphant Paul, sweeping before him all opposition, internal and external, to the true gospel of Jesus Christ, was inherited from the Reformation, when Paul was the instrument for purification of ecclesiastical abuses. In that situation, nothing less than one who had triumphed in the preaching of the gospel could be contemplated. We have arrived here at a different kind of picture, however, one not of a triumphant missionary who carried all opponents before him, but of one who was involved in the controversies of the early church, and who in the end was less triumphant than triumphed over. While it is not the usual picture, and seems something less than a pleasant, or even a satisfactory, portrait of the career of Paul, the apostle to the Gentiles, it is nevertheless an account which, I would urge, adheres more closely to a careful and critical interpretation of the evidence we have than do other, more romantic accounts.

Obviously, we cannot conclude that Paul's defeat in Antioch meant that he was eliminated from the memory of the church. His inclusion in Acts as a hero of the faith, his letters within the canonical New Testament which make up a large fraction of the material contained in it, the other letters composed in his name both within the canon and outside of it, the favorable mention given of him, if not of his letters, in 2 Peter 3:15–16, the favorable recollection of him in *1 Clement* 5.5–7—these data (and other, similar data in the early church Fathers) attest to the fact that Paul was indeed remembered as apostle, missionary, and martyr of the faith. Yet it was his reputation, particularly as martyred apostle, more than his teachings themselves, that was remembered. To that extent the dispute at Antioch meant that an interpretation of the faith other than Paul's would become normative, and would remain normative for some fourteen centuries!

THE REMEMBERED PAUL

The way Paul was remembered is shown with particular clarity in the account in Acts, where the Paul we know from his letters, that is, Paul with his particular theological perspective, is replaced by a Paul willing to compromise his view of the relationship of law and faithfulness to God in Christ in order to preserve the unity of the faith and the leading role of the Christian authorities in Jerusalem. In Acts, Paul is pictured as precisely the kind of theologian who could give wholehearted support to the Apostolic Decree. He is also pictured as one who, although he might part from Barnabas in the gentile missionary enterprise, nevertheless at the end would return to Jerusalem and dutifully subordinate himself to the authorities there (Acts 21:20–26).[21]

Again, the Pastoral Epistles (1 and 2 Timothy, Titus) and the seven Catholic Epistles (James, 1 and 2 Peter, 1, 2 and 3 John, Jude) in the New Testament, as well as the writings commonly called the "Apostolic Fathers," tend to show by the way they write of the Christian faith that they now understand it more as a system of doctrine and especially an ethical code than as an acknowledgment of God's redemptive act in Jesus Christ by which God opened the way through faith to reconciliation with himself.

Paul and Peter

More specifically, relative to the dispute at Antioch between Peter and Paul about the conditions necessary if fellowship between Jewish and gentile Christians is to be possible (i.e., the Apostolic Decree),

SOME HISTORICAL CONCLUSIONS

there is evidence that this dispute between the two apostles continued to play a role in the later history of doctrinal disputes. Moreover, there is evidence of the influence of the Apostolic Decree on the understanding of the Christian faith far into the second and third centuries, where elements from it become the major tenets which distinguish the Christian from the pagan position. That is true even where, long after the destruction of Jerusalem in A.D. 70 and the end of an influential Christian body there, the incorporation of elements of Judaism into Christian belief and practice continued to be perceived as a threat. A look at the evidence is instructive.

Gal. 2:11–13. There is first of all the problem of the dispute between Peter and Paul, recorded in Gal. 2:11–13. We have already seen Luke's exaltation of a Paul rather unlike the apostle we meet in his letters. But it is also probable that the evident equation of Peter and Paul as apostles in the book of Acts (both are traveling missionaries; both work about the same number of miracles of very similar kinds; both preach the gospel to Jews and Gentiles) grows out of an attempt to minimize the effects of that dispute between them.[22] The favorable comments about Paul made by the author of a letter purporting to be written by Peter (i.e., 2 Peter 3:15–16) may also represent an early and deliberate attempt to play down the effects of the dispute between these key figures in the history of the earliest church.[23]

Recollection of that dispute did not disappear with the composition of the canonical New Testament books, however. Its influence made itself felt into the second century and beyond. Marcion, for example, appears to have justified his preference for Paul by pointing to Paul's condemnation of Peter (Gal. 2:11). Marcion concluded from that condemnation that Peter was ignorant of true Christianity (cf. also Gal. 2:14).[24] This view was also shared by the Valentinians who held that Paul was the superior apostle due to Peter's imperfection, an imperfection laid bare by Paul's condemnation of him.[25]

Far more widespread, however, than the evaluation of the opposition to Peter in favor of Paul in light of the dispute at Antioch was the evaluation of the opposition to Paul in favor of Peter, and, unlike those who favored Paul, those who favored Peter came to be recognized in later times as those who were right, i.e., "orthodox." Evidence for the latter evaluation may well be found as early as the canonical Gospel of Matthew, where some have cited the polemical language of Matt. 16:17–19 as evidence that this evangelist intended to combat claims made on behalf of some other apostolic authority. The self-exaltation by Paul of his authority in Gal. 2:11–13 has then been cited as the authority Matthew is combating.[26]

Pseudo-Clementine Literature. Perhaps the chief source of the anti-Pauline polemic in the second century and beyond is the Pseudo-Clementine literature, and the *Kerygma(ta) Petrou,* a postulated source-document which may underlie the Pseudo-Clementine *Homilies.*[27] Here Paul's apostleship appears to be attacked under the guise of an attack on Simon Magus, who is described as a missionary to the Gentiles (*Hom.* 2.17) and as one whose teaching does not agree with that of James of Jerusalem (*Hom.* 11.35). Simon is further pictured as one who argues that (his) apostleship on the basis of a vision is superior to that (Peter's) based on sensory perception (*Hom.* 17.13). He is also portrayed as having stood in opposition to Peter and as having said that Peter was condemned (*Hom.* 17.19). The references here to Paul's conversion, and to Gal. 2:11–13, are clear.[28]

There is, moreover, evidence that Luke's understanding of the resolution of the difficulties between Jewish and gentile Christians, evidence epitomized in the Apostolic Decree, triumphed in the later church. That evidence shows more clearly than any opposition expressed against one or the other of the figures in the dispute, Peter and Paul, the extent to which the Antioch dispute ended in the virtual disappearance of the kind of gospel Paul had preached as missionary to the Gentiles.

Again, the Pseudo-Clementines witness the extent to which this way of understanding the Christian faith assumed ascendancy. Careful examination of the literature shows how again and again, the essence of the faith is expressed in terms that reflect the Apostolic Decree.[29] *Homily* 10.8, for example, commands abstention from food offered to idols (*eidolothytos*[30]); from eating dead carcasses, animals suffocated (*pniktos*) or killed by wild beasts; from eating blood (*aima*); and from sexual impurity (*porneia*). Similarly, *Homily* 7.4 lists as things pleasing to God abstention from the table of demons (= idolatry, *eidolothytos*), not eating dead flesh or blood (*aima*), being washed from all pollution (in context = *porneia*), and observing the golden rule, which in the Codex Bezae text of Acts 15:20 is substituted for the prohibition against eating things strangled.

In a number of other instances, a series of ethical admonitions are introduced with elements clearly derived from the Apostolic Decree.

In *Homily* 8.19, an angel sent to speak to demons begins his description of those who worship them as people who participate at their (i.e., the demons') tables (= idolatry, *eidōlothytos*), who shed blood (*aima* as moral category; murder), and who eat the flesh of animals that were torn by wild beasts or that were suffocated (*pniktos*). In *Homily* 8.23 a list of forbidden activities begins with prohibition of idolatry (*eidōlothytos*), murder (*aima* as moral category), and adultery (*porneia*). *Homily* 4.36 begins its list of things that pollute the soul and body with a listing of idolatry (*eidōlothys*) and eating blood (*aima*) or anything strangled (*pniktos*).

Justin Martyr. Such data are not limited to the Pseudo-Clementine materials however. Justin Martyr, in his *Dialogue with Trypho*, notes that those who follow the crucified Jesus would "rather endure every torture and pain, even death itself, than worship idols, or eat meat sacrificed to idols."[31] When in the next chapter (35), Trypho claims to know of Christians who claim there is no harm in eating meats sacrificed to idols, it may be that he is referring to Christians who followed Paul's advice to the Corinthian Christians about meat purchased in the marketplace (e.g., 1 Cor. 9:19–21). Justin Martyr's condemnation of them would then be further evidence of conflict between those who followed Paul and those who accepted the Apostolic Decree. At this period of time, and in this context, however, it is more likely that what Trypho has in mind here are Christians who thought they could continue to take part in ceremonies dedicated to idols, a practice Paul condemned among the Corinthian Christians (e.g., 1 Cor. 10:14, 20–21). Such a situation would not point to conflict among Christians of Pauline and Petrine persuasion. The same prohibition against idolatry and eating meat sacrificed to idols is also contained in *Didache* 6.3.

Such a prohibition against idolatry, however, was so pervasive among early Christians, including Paul (cf. Rom. 1:23, where Paul identified idolatry as the beginning of human rebellion against God), that it could be considered to exist apart from any reinforcement from the Apostolic Decree. Such is not the case, however, in the matter of the widespread prohibition against eating blood. That is strictly a Jewish prohibition—Gentiles ate blood as a regular practice—and its prohibition among Christians is in all probability derived from the Apostolic Decree. Tertullian, for example, says Christians refrain from eating animals that have been strangled or that die "lest we be in any way contaminated with blood, even if it is hidden in the flesh" (*Apology* 9.13).[32] There is a similar horror of consuming the blood of animals expressed in Minucius Felix (30.6), as there is in Eusebius (*Ecclesiastical History* 5.1.26).

That kind of prohibition of the consumption of animal blood is in no way limited to those areas where Jewish Christianity exercised an influence. In fact, Justin Martyr totally rejects any attempt to introduce elements of Jewish faith or practice into the gentile Christian community. Christian Jews may continue such practices if they wish, Justin concedes, but if they urge gentile Christians to follow Jewish practices, those Jewish Christians would forfeit salvation in Christ (*Dialogue with Trypho* 47; cf. also 46). Similarly, Tertullian, discussing the relationship of Christianity to Judaism, denies any similarities of practice between them (*Apology* 21.2)[33] The influence of the Apostolic Decree, therefore, was strong even in those areas where there was no sympathy to Jewish Christianity, and no inclination to introduce Jewish practices into the Christian faith. The Apostolic Decree, it would appear, was remembered and followed as a routine matter of Christian practice long after salvation by grace through faith ceased to be regarded as the touchstone of the Christian faith.[34]

IDEAL OF UNITY

Thus that elusive unity, for which Peter yearned and which Paul sought to achieve, which James attempted to preserve and which Luke labored to portray in his account of the early church—that unity in fact was not achieved. It was as much an ideal in relation to the earliest Christian communities as it remains an ideal in relation to the Christian churches of this day. That early unity existed, and continues to exist, only in the optimistic historical imagination of scholars who cannot bring themselves to believe that Paul really lost the dispute in Antioch, a loss with lasting results for the Christian church; or who cannot bring themselves to believe that Peter, after his right hand offered to Paul in agreement with his apostolic mission to the Gentiles, could have betrayed Paul by siding with the emissaries from James, thus committing his prestige to a denial of the validity of Paul's theological position. Perhaps the present and the future of the church, and its goal of unity, would be better served by recognizing the situation for what it was, rather than hiding it beneath the patina of an overly optimistic historical imagination.[35]

8
HISTORICAL REPORTING AND
THE PURPOSE OF ACTS

The results of our study have done nothing if not call into question the historical reliability of the narratives contained in Acts, as that reliability would be judged by any meaningful modern standard of historical investigation. That must inevitably raise two questions, the one concerning the validity of such an analysis, and the second concerning the value of Acts as a canonical writing. If the narratives we read in Acts turn out not to be accurate historical records, again in any useful modern sense, of the events those narratives report, then of what value is Acts, whether as a document relevant to the faith of the Christian church or as a writing useful for learning about the history of the early church? Is not the inevitable result of the kind of historical investigation undertaken in these pages to discredit Acts, and finally to dissuade anyone from taking it seriously? To consider that kind of objection with the care it deserves, it is necessary to examine carefully the purpose of Acts, beginning with that purpose as the author himself has defined it.

ACCURACY OR INACCURACY?

The judgment that any investigation that produces results such as this one must inevitably render Acts useless for the church rests on the presupposition that the value of Acts stands or falls with the historical accuracy, judged once more in terms of modern historiography, which can be assigned to it. This question is often phrased in such terms as: Can the Gospel according to Luke and the Acts of the Apostles be trusted? That question will then often be answered by pointing out that Luke "explicitly claims to be writing an 'orderly account,'" and that therefore unless his historical accuracy can be proved, the narratives cannot "be trusted." Needless to say, such an argument will then be devoted to "proving" Luke's "accuracy" in what he reports.[1]

Much if not all of that "proof" will take the form of pointing to the vast sweep of geography and the large numbers of persons mentioned in Luke-Acts, and to all those places where Luke is historically accurate. If notice is taken at all of the notorious problems of historical inaccuracies which have been identified in Acts (as well as in Luke), it will usually be argued that they have really been shown by "archaeology and historical research"[2] not to have been inaccuracies after all.

Yet even a brief survey of only some of those problems will indicate that they are serious ones, and that they cannot simply be dismissed or ignored by anyone who wants to claim historical accuracy for all narrative details in Luke. Among such problems are the following: (1) the otherwise unknown, and almost certainly misplaced, census which Luke reports to have taken place under Quirinius when he was governor of Syria (Luke 2:1–2; Acts 5:37); (2) the demonstrably inaccurate chronological reference to the apparently dual high-priesthood of Annas (A.D. 6–15) and Caiaphas (A.D. 18–36); (3) a pattern of high-priesthood unknown apart from this reference to Annas and Caiaphas, who in fact were separated by three years and three other high priests (Luke 3:2); and (4) the (historically reversed) order of appearance of Theudas (ca. A.D. 44–46) and Judas the Galilean (ca. A.D. 6; Acts 5:36–37).

There are other problems as well, consisting of references to data which create difficulties for anyone wishing to take all historical material reported in Luke-Acts as "factually reliable" in the modern sense. There is, for one example, the presence of the cohort *Italica* in Caesarea Maritima in the time of Herod Agrippa (Acts 10:1), a stationing of Roman troops impossible in the period prior to Herod's death (but probably the case when Luke was writing); Luke has apparently assumed that conditions prevailing in his day must also have prevailed during the period about which he was writing. To cite one final example, there is the geographical problem created by the (reversed) mention of Jesus' "passing along between" or "through the midst of" (the meaning is uncertain) "Samaria and Galilee" on "the way to Jerusalem" (Luke 17:11) apparently on the supposition that Galilee lies south of Samaria.[3] No amount of tinkering with the text, or calling into question the present state of the historiographer's art can wish away those problems of what by any modern standard could only be classed as inaccurate historical detail in Luke-Acts.

Does the existence of such inaccuracies then diminish, if not eliminate, the value of Luke-Acts? Only if the basic, not to say sole, purpose of Luke was to write an "accurate" (as defined in popular understanding of historiography: an account of events "as they really happened")[4] chronological account of the development of the early church. Yet one must ask whether that really was Luke's purpose, as James Montgomery Boice assumes. Does Luke's reference to his desire to write an "orderly account" really mean "orderly" in the sense of "historically accurate?"[5] Fortunately, Luke tells us in Luke 1:1–4 what he intended to do in his two-volume work, and a careful analysis of those verses at the beginning of Luke will help us answer the question of historical reporting and the purpose of Acts.

LUKE'S PREFACE (LUKE 1:1–4)

Following Hellenistic literary convention, and indeed imitating its style (the bulk of Luke's writing, on the other hand, follows more closely the Greek constructions of the Septuagint [LXX] rather than any Hellenistic literary sensitivities), Luke prefaces his first book, the Gospel, with a statement of intention. There is a preface to the second volume, Acts, but the opening verses of that narrative ("In the first book, O Theophilus, . . .") serve more to tie the second volume to the first than to introduce it as a separate piece of literature. It is therefore not so clearly set off from the story that ensues, and it does not follow so clearly the Hellenistic literary customs for an introduction as do the opening verses of the Gospel. For that reason, it is clear that what Luke says in Luke 1:1–4 was intended to stand for both volumes. It is the words Luke chose, however, rather than the style he imitated, that help determine his purpose, and so we will concentrate our attention on the key words in that literary introduction.

(1) Inasmuch as many have undertaken to compile a narrative (*anataxasthai diēgēsin*) of the things which have been accomplished (*tōn peplērophorēmenōn . . . pragmatōn*) among us, (2) just as they were delivered (*paredosan*) to us by those who from the beginning were eyewitnesses and ministers of the word, (3) it seemed good to me also, having followed all things closely (*akribōs*) for some time past, to write an orderly account (*kathexēs . . . grapsai*) for you, most excellent Theophilus, (4) that you may know the truth (*hina epignōs . . . tēn asphaleian*) concerning the things of which you have been informed (*katēchēthēs*).

(Luke 1:1–4)

Perhaps most important in the first verse is the fact that Luke chooses a verb meaning "fulfill" (*plērophoreō*) to describe the events ("things which have been accomplished") he is about to record, rather than the more common, and less theologically loaded, verb "occur" (*ginomai*). The "events" (*pragmata*) therefore about which he is going to write did not simply "occur," they were "carried to fulfillment." Now that choice of language is either hopelessly pretentious, using a complex word where a simple one would do, or (something Luke's skill with Greek makes more likely on the face of it) Luke wanted to say something about what he understood those events to mean. The word "fulfill" points to the difference between Luke and those historians who intend primarily to chronicle events accurately, namely, the fact that for Luke the "events" he is going to narrate serve a theological rather than a historical purpose. They are intended to show how Christianity, in its connection with and continuation of Judaism, is the fulfillment of God's history with his chosen people. Thus Luke's historical concern serves a theological end: The events he is to narrate will show how things foreshadowed in the biblical history of Israel have now come to fruition. That such is Luke's intent is then confirmed both by his language, patterned as it is after that of the Greek Old Testament (LXX), and by his many references to Old Testament passages as fulfillments which in their original context had no predictive quality about them.[6]

The first thing the reader must recognize about Luke's material, therefore, is that he is not recounting the story of Jesus and of his followers simply, or even primarily, as a Hellenistic historian, concerned to "get it right."[7] Rather, Luke's "historical" narrative is intended primarily to serve theological ends. His historical intention is therefore clearly subordinated to a theological purpose, and to miss that will be to misunderstand Luke-Acts from the outset.

Nor does Luke call what he is writing *historia*, a word used to identify historical narratives as early as Herodotus and as recently as Plutarch, probably a contemporary of Luke. Rather, Luke chooses the more neutral *diēgēsis*, "narrative," a term which would not call up expectations in the reader about historical procedures that would not represent Luke's intention. Again, when Luke in v. 1 describes the kind of task he is undertaking, he uses the aorist infinitive of the verb *anatassō* (*anataxasthai*), which means "set in order." Luke thus claims that what he is doing is similar to what "many" have done who have "set their hand to constructing an orderly narrative."[8] What is meant by "orderly" we will examine in detail in relation to v. 3.

In v. 2, Luke tells us the source of his information. Here too he is indebted to others who have gone before, as he was in undertaking this narrative form. Luke is dependent on the "traditions" (the Greek verb "delivered" or "handed on," *paradidōmi*, is the technical term for the transmission of traditions; cf. 1 Cor. 11:23; 15:3) of the original eyewitnesses of these events. These people, who were with Jesus from the beginning (cf. Acts 1:21–22a), and who were the first preachers of the gospel, are the ones upon whom Luke depends for what he is going to write. In that way he makes it clear from the outset that he will not be relying on his own memory of these events to get them in the proper historical order, even if that were his intention. What he is going to "narrate" in "orderly fashion" are the traditions of the eyewitnesses. We have seen ample evidence of the fragmentary nature of some of these traditions. Luke thus belongs to the second generation of Christians. If those who wrote narratives before him were these eyewitnesses, or if, as is more likely, those narratives were put together by followers of the eyewitnesses, then Luke belongs to the third generation of Christians:

first generation: eyewitnesses
second generation: the first composers of narratives from eyewitness traditions
third generation: Luke who uses such narratives as a model

In v. 3 we find another word referring to "order," this time an adverb (*kathexēs*), modifying the verb "to write." We are now in a better position to ask what Luke meant by "order" than we were in v. 1, since he has now told us more about his intention in his literary work. What he intends to do, based on his careful scrutiny of those traditions that reach back to the beginning of the period he is going to cover and that come from the eyewitnesses themselves,[9] is to arrange those traditions "in an orderly way." Clearly, we need to understand what "orderly" meant to Luke if we are to be clear on what he is writing, and whether or not we can expect "historical accuracy," as we tend generally to define it,[10] to have been one of his principal concerns.

Ancient authors, even those such as Tacitus or Suetonius who wrote history,[11] recognized other ways to order a narrative than simply chronological. Charles Talbert has identified five purposes for which ancient biographies were written, and none was for the purpose of providing accurate chronological information.[12] Thus, "order," even in an avowedly historical writing, would not necessarily connote chronological order, nor need it in Luke's case. Indeed, as Luke himself has announced (Acts 1:8), his principal order is to be geographical, not temporal, and he then develops his narrative in blocks that reflect this geographical intention, beginning in Jerusalem and moving progressively to Rome, dealing in detail with an area and then not returning to describe in any detail any further events that took place there.[13] He handles characters in a similar way, dealing first with Peter (chaps. 1—12) and then with Paul (chaps. 13—28).[14]

Yet we are not dependent on the general meaning of "order" in Hellenistic literature, or on a general discussion of Lukan literary constructions or techniques to determine what meaning that word bears in Luke 1:3. Luke uses the same word for "order" (*kathexēs*) in Acts 11:4 to characterize Peter's recitation of some events of which he had been a part. Peter's "orderly" recitation is of an event that had already been narrated in Acts 10, namely, the conversion of Cornelius and his family. This gives us an ideal opportunity to examine in what sense Luke meant *kathexēs*, since we can check the "orderly" account (Acts 11:4–17) against the earlier narrative of the events Peter is reciting (10:9–33). A careful examination proves illuminating, and makes clear that "orderly" does not mean "chronological" or even "events in the same order."

The narrative in Acts 10 tells us that (1) Peter was near Joppa, (2) he went to the housetop to pray, (3) he became hungry, and (4) he fell into a trance (vv. 9–10). The "orderly" account in Acts 11(*a*) puts him in Joppa (no housetop mentioned), and (*b*) reports that while praying he fell into a trance; here the location (1; *a*) and order of events (3, 4; *b*) have been changed. In the narrative, Peter refuses the command to eat by saying that he has never eaten anything common and unclean (10:14); in the account he replies that nothing common and unclean has ever entered his mouth (11:8). There is a slight difference in accent; the account is even more emphatic than the narrative about Peter's state of *kashrut*.

Again, in the narrative, (1) the men from (2) Cornelius (3) appear while Peter is reflecting on the meaning of the vision (10:17). In the account, (*a*) the men appear (*b*) at the "very moment" the vision concludes (11:11). Here again there are changes in chronological and other details. Cornelius is never named in the account and all the detail in the narrative about his vision (10:1–8) is omitted in the account; there he is only "the man."

Further, in the narrative, Peter (1) invites the men from Cornelius to be guests in the house, (2) departs with them the next day, and (3) they arrive the following day (10:23–24). In the account, Peter (a) goes with them as soon as they have appeared and (b) enters Cornelius's house (11:12). Here the difference is considerable, with the account reporting events as seemingly instantaneous which in the narrative took three days. Finally, most of the detail in the narrative about what happened in Cornelius's house (10:25–48) is simply omitted in the account (11:15–16).

Now of course, for those who know the narrative, the changes in the account are quite understandable and cause the reader no difficulty. But that is not the point. The point is that Luke could call such an account, playing fast and loose as it did with chronological and other details, an "orderly" (*kathexēs*) account, the same word used in Luke 1:3. As an account of the "history" of the events in 10:1–48 it leaves much to be desired; historical details are changed, motivations are left unexplained, and necessary detail is omitted. Yet the account is shaped for the situation in which Peter finds himself, and it makes his point about not being able to withstand God (11:17) so well that opposition is silenced (11:18). That tells us a good deal about what Luke means by an "orderly account": if Peter's account is not good "history," it is an excellent defense of his actions, which was appropriate for the situation in which he found himself (11:2–3). Rather clearly, it was in this sense that Luke felt Peter's account was "orderly": It was appropriate for the task at hand and accomplished the desired end. It would therefore seem justified to conclude that "orderly" in Luke 1:3 means "systematically," that is, in a given literary (rather than historical) order which is appropriate for the task he has set himself.

The fourth verse of the Lukan prologue discusses just what that desired end of the narrative was which Luke was writing, and shows us to what situation his "orderly account" was appropriate. Here the key word is *asphaleian*, put in the emphatic (final) position at the end of this long and periodic sentence (vv. 1–4).[15] It means "assurance" or "guarantee." The narrative was thus written so "Theophilus" may "recognize" (*epignōs*) what is certain or assured of those events about which he has already received oral instruction (*katēchēthēs*). Theophilus is thus not receiving information for the first time; he is now to find out what he can recognize as assured among those events about which he had heard. To put it in the framework of the prologue, what Theophilus is about to read in this "orderly account" is a narrative ap-

73

propriate for the task at hand: to give him assurance about the meaning of the traditions of which he has already heard. Chronological accuracy is hardly the kind of assurance Luke provides or Theophilus seeks; it is rather assurance that these events fulfill God's word given to his chosen people,[16] and that thus Jesus is assuredly God's message of salvation to Theophilus and others like him who repent of their sins, are baptized (Acts 3:38), and acknowledge that there is no other name "under heaven . . . by which we must be saved" (Acts 4:12). It was to meet the need of Theophilus for such assurance that Luke was writing, and it was in that sense that Luke set out to create an "orderly," that is, "appropriate" account.

9

REFLECTIONS ON SOME UNTRADITIONAL CONCLUSIONS

We have noted that many people interpret the "orderly account" Luke says he set out to write in terms of a chronological order. We also saw evidence to show rather clearly that this was not Luke's purpose in writing. But if Acts is not the history it appears to be, of what value is it? If historic events did not occur as portrayed in Acts—and we have seen good reason to believe many of them did not—of what value is Acts to the Christian community?

We have already implied an answer. Now we need to be explicit. The value of Acts lies not in its detailed historical accuracy, or in the reliability of its sequential chronological reporting. The value of Acts lies in the theological points the author wishes to make about the way the early church developed. Some of those are: the guidance provided by the Holy Spirit, even when the mission appeared to be hindered (cf. 16:6); the significance of the conversion of Gentiles; the intimate relationship between Judaism and Christianity, affirming both God's choice of the Jews to be his people and God's guidance of the Christian community as the heir to Israel's promises. In these and other theological points are to be found the materials of value in Luke's reflections on the progress of the early church. One must note well: the value of Acts lies in the theological reflections embodied in it, not in historical information about the early church, interesting and at times as accurate as that may be.

When one recognizes in this the value of Acts, one will have made a judgment about Acts that is no different from the judgment scholars have made about the value of the Gospel Luke wrote, or for that matter, about any of the Gospels. Their value lies not in their historically accurate details, nor in the reliability of their chronological se-

75

quences;[1] a comparison of the Gospels will show how they vary in these matters. Yet the Gospel of Luke was written under the same program and for the same purpose as Acts, as their prologues show. Why then should we expect a different treatment of the material in the latter than in the former? In both, Luke must rely on traditions, and in both he arranges them to provide Theophilus with the assurance he needs about the matters dealt with in his oral instruction in the faith.

The truth to be found in Acts therefore is badly served if it is limited to, or even judged by the quality of, its historically accurate details. Its value for the Christian community of faith does not lie there. It lies in the theological reflections Luke has provided his readers, informing them that the early church was not primarily a social or political phenomenon, but was rather a community called into being by God's Son. That community was then continually guided by God's Spirit, and shaped in such a way as to display to sinful humanity a foretaste of that glorious day when God's rule would be publicly manifested. At that final manifestation, all humanity would know the truth about God and about the community of faith that he had called together in the name of his Son.[2]

Two further questions arise, and they are linked together. One of Luke's theological points concerned the unity of the early church, something we have seen not to have been so monolithic, nor even very closely related to his portrait of it. Do not the results of this kind of study therefore destroy part of Luke's specifically theological program, thus making even that program of little value for the Christian community? Second, and related to it, is the question: How could, or why would, Luke have distorted the truth, when he portrayed a unity that in fact did not exist as he portrayed it, particularly as it affected the relationship between Paul and the authorities in Jerusalem?

Let us begin with the second question. I do not believe Luke knowingly distorted the evidence he had about the early church. I agree with those scholars who assert that Luke did not have copies of Paul's letters. Indeed, absence of any mention of Paul writing letters may mean Luke was not even aware that Paul had written any. When Luke set his hand to his announced task, he was confronted with a mass of traditions, as he himself said in his prologue to Luke. He also possessed, along with the traditions about Jesus, a framework of the career of Jesus in the form of Mark's Gospel, which he used and adapted to fit his theological purposes. He did not, so far as scholars have been able to determine, possess a similar framework of the story of the early church. Here he had to deduce the order of events from the traditions (much as Mark had to do when he created his Gospel from traditions about Jesus), and from traditions that were, it appears, often incomplete and fragmentary.

One would face the same situation were one to attempt to write an account of the origin and development of the gentile mission in the early church if all one had were the Pauline letters.[3] Some periods would be clear; for example, Paul's travels in and around Corinth (and Achaia), or around Ephesus (and Asia), which are reported in the Corinthian correspondence (although even here there are problems reconciling what Paul says about his travels in 1 Corinthians with what he says about them in 2 Corinthians). Locating other letters in time and place, such letters as Philippians, for instance, would be another matter altogether. One's only recourse, were one truly intent on creating an "orderly" narrative, would be to make some assumptions about the way Paul's general career had proceeded (perhaps a general movement from east to west, with centers of activity in Damascus, Antioch, Ephesus, and Corinth), assumptions derived, quite naturally, from the evidence one had, however limited and incomplete it might be. One would then be forced to fit the remaining evidence into the framework one had constructed at those points where, based on one's assumptions, it appeared to fit most appropriately. If one erred, it would not be because of a desire to defraud, or because one was unintelligent; it would simply be due to lack of information. If further evidence about Paul were discovered (the "Letter to the Laodiceans" mentioned in Col. 4:16, for example), one could then further refine and correct one's account of his missionary career.

Such is the case, it seems to me, that Luke faced when he set out to write the second part of his account of Jesus and his earliest followers. Faced with a number of traditions, many fragmentary and disconnected, Luke had to make certain assumptions, based of course on the traditions he had, about the way the early church developed. It is just those assumptions scholars have called Luke's "biases" or "tendencies." They are the assumptions that Luke drew from his traditions, and that he then used to organize those traditions into a coherent narrative.

If it were possible to find additional evidence about certain events in the life of the early church, evidence that Luke did not have, so that he had instead to rely on his assumptions, the possibility would arise that one could show, on the basis of that new evidence, that Luke's assumptions had, at that particular point, led him astray.

That, it seems to me, is exactly the situation in which we find ourselves in the case of Acts, since we possess in the form of Paul's letters additional evidence that Luke, by all indications, did not possess. It is this evidence from Paul himself that we have brought to bear in our analysis of Luke's account of the early church. It has led us to conclude that, based on this "new" evidence, we can see some things that Luke, lacking the evidence contained in those letters, could not see. In those instances where Luke lacked that evidence, he was forced to give coherence to his narrative on the basis of his assumptions about the development of the earliest Christian community.

That insight into the way Luke operated also provides us with the answer to our first question: Luke portrayed the unity of the early church in more monolithic terms than in fact was the case. Here again, Luke was aware of the enormous desire within the Christian community for the unity of the church, a desire clearly shared by Paul when, despite the personal danger to himself, he took his offering to the authorities in Jerusalem in a final effort to achieve unity between gentile and Jewish Christian movements. Luke also was aware that the community was not hostage to political or social forces that affected its development in ways unanticipated by or counter to God's will. Rather, its existence was moving precisely in accordance with God's redemptive plan made known in his son Jesus. Luke also knew that an attempt had been made to find a compromise between the dissident factions of Jews and Gentiles, namely, the Apostolic Decree, which, as we saw, exerted its influence long after Luke had written and passed from the scene.

Based on that information, Luke assumed the desire for a unified church had been accomplished within the first decades of the existence of the church. That assumption proved not to be the case, as Luke would also have known had he possessed, for example, the Letters of John or the Gospel of Matthew, with their evidence of the fractured nature of the earliest Christian community. That lack of evidence on Luke's part does not nullify his basic conviction that the early Christian community must be understood as more than just a social or political movement. Nor does it make the unification of the followers of Jesus Christ any less imperative now than Luke understood it to be in his time, or in the time of the very earliest church.

CONCLUSIONS

What all of this indicates is that even with the canon, and the inspiration that brought it into existence and caused it to be collected and preserved, the Christian community still walks by faith and not by sight. There is no firm handhold for the Christian community, not even a historical one, other than faith that the crucified and risen Jesus was the redemptive act of the God who created the world and intends the rescue of his rebellious creatures.

Finally, what of Paul? As we have pictured his career, he was not the conquering theological hero of the early church which Protestants have made of him since the Reformation. Rather, he has appeared to be the one who lost in the struggle to influence the theological mind of the early church. Although that community preserved his memory and his theology within the canon, it interpreted his letters in ways totally differently from the ways he had apparently intended them to be understood. This simply shows that if Paul lost the battle, he did not lose the war! His influence was preserved within the canon, which has continued to exercise its critical function on the theologizing of the church down through the centuries of its existence. Like a prophet in her midst, the canon has never allowed the church the comfortable sleep of the theologically complacent, but has continually challenged her to take into account those new dimensions of the faith that unfold from a careful consideration of every part of that canon.

In light of Paul's own letters, could one find a more appropriate portrayal than the one we have drawn? Surely it is an appropriate portrayal of the one who, denied three times his prayer for deliverance from his "messenger of Satan," learned from that that the Lord's power was made perfect in Paul's weakness (2 Cor. 12:7–9). Surely it is an appropriate portrayal of the one who, for the sake of Christ, confessed himself content with "weakness, insults, hardships, persecutions, and calamities," all on the basis of the fact that his true strength lay in his weakness (2 Cor. 12:10). Surely it is an appropriate portrayal of the Paul who claimed to his Philippian readers that for whatever motive evangelization was carried on, whether to support or undermine him, so long as Christ was proclaimed he was content (Phil. 1:15–17). It may well be that Paul's language in that passage is a far more direct and literal description of his experience as a missionary than students of Paul have realized or been willing to admit; there may actually have been Christians who "proclaim[ed] Christ out of partisanship, not sincerely but thinking to afflict me in my imprisonment" (v. 17). What more literal description could one want of those who had caused Barnabas to withdraw from partnership with him in the gospel to the Gentiles?

If the Paul we have portrayed was a less triumphant figure in the early history of the church than one has come to expect, that in itself may cause those who now read his letters to take more seriously his claim that his only source of strength was Christ, whatever the (historical) circumstances may have been in which he found himself. It may cause his readers to gain greater insight into the one who affirmed that his only boast was of the things that made clear his own weakness. A victorious Paul, who carried all before him in theological triumph, or a Paul who knew his own weaknesses and defeat, and found in them the strength of Christ crucified—which is the more accurate portrayal of the Paul we find in his own letters?

Paul himself answers that question:

> We are fools for Christ's sake. . . . We are weak . . . we are held in dishonor . . . we are ill-clad and buffeted and homeless . . . when reviled we bless; when persecuted, we endure; when slandered, we try to conciliate; we have become, and are now, as the refuse of the world, the offscouring of all things.
>
> (1 Cor. 4:10–13)

We must begin to recognize in those phrases not the perhaps pardonable overstatements of one whose zeal tended to outrun his propriety when he spoke of himself. For Paul to have written such words in any other than a literal meaning to his converts would have been to open himself to the charge of a most pernicious form of self-praise.[4] Rather, we must recognize there a sober and literal description of Paul's actual life as a missionary. To recognize in that figure the Paul of history is to begin to understand what he endured as one whose unshakable missionary resolve it was "to know nothing among you except Jesus Christ and him crucified" (1 Cor. 2:2).

Nor can we understand all such references to his own difficulties and defeats as an apostle solely on the basis of opposition from without. Although his being "utterly, unbearably crushed" in Asia (2 Cor. 1:8) may have been the work of opponents outside the Christian fellowship, the pain inflicted on him in Corinth, both in his presence there (2 Cor. 2:1–4) and in his absence (2 Cor. 10:10), was clearly inflicted by others within the Christian fellowship. Although the problem that caused him first to pause in Galatia was the result of external forces, in this case weakness due to illness (Gal. 4:13), the problems reflected in the remainder of his letter to the church there were due to other Christian preachers who opposed what Paul took to be the heart of the gospel (Gal. 2:6–9; cf. 5:2–12; cf. 2 Cor. 11:4 for a similar description of Christian opponents). Again, Paul's "thorn in the flesh," given to keep him "from being too elated" is often understood as a bodily ailment. Yet it is also called a "messenger of Satan" and results not only in "weaknesses" but also in "insults, hardships, persecutions, and calamities," hardly the result only of a bodily ailment. Those results reflect precisely the kind of hardship Paul underwent in his apostolic activity (cf. 2 Cor. 11:23–27). Even if one may not want to identify that "messenger of Satan" as a specific individual,[5] the description of the messenger's results opens the possibility of understanding the messenger to be those Christians who have made it a practice to oppose Paul.

Furthermore, to see Paul otherwise than we have portrayed him is to drive a wedge between his life and his theology in a manner quite contrary to the way he himself understood them. It is to imagine him as belittling himself for his difficulties, yet all the while moving from theological triumph to theological triumph. His letters simply do not bear out that kind of interpretation. Clearly, when he affirms to the Galatians that it is no longer he who continues to live but Christ (2:20), he means to affirm that his life and his theology are one, a point confirmed in the very next verse with its claim that Paul does not nullify God's grace (v. 21). Life and theology are one for Paul, and to understand them in different terms is simply to misunderstand Paul. To say that a theology of the cross precedes a theology of glory in Paul is as much to describe the life he lived as the theology he proclaimed.

Even in his life, therefore, Paul lived by grace (despite his defeats in his career as apostle of Christ) rather than by works (victories in that career). He had nothing to boast of but weakness, defeat, and peril, and the picture of Paul we have seen in these pages in fact reflects that. Those who rejected his doctine of grace therefore must of necessity have rejected his life as an apostle, something for which we have seen ample evidence. Again, Paul did not hold one thing in his theology and experience another in his life. He was not forced to affirm a string of personal defeats despite his victories in his missionary enterprise for Christ lest his life seem to contradict his theology. Rather, his theology allowed him to affirm that not he but Christ lived in him, because his life was shaped along the same contours as his theology. God had called him to serve a savior who had died on a cross in agony; a triumphant apostle of such a one would have been a contradiction in terms.

If there was finally to be a triumph, and Paul never doubted for a moment that there would be (e.g., Phil. 2:10–11), it would be the triumph of grace, and it would be the triumph of Christ. Yet even here the analogy of Christ's death and resurrection Paul frequently applies to his own ministry implies Paul's lack of theological victories. While Paul experiences the reality of the crucifixion now, he will enjoy the reality of the resurrection only in the future.[6] The reality of that crucifixion is often portrayed in precisely the kind of terms in which Paul portrays the difficulties he experiences as an apostle (e.g., 2 Cor. 4:8–10). Therefore, it is precisely his difficulties and defeats as an apostle that let him participate in Christ's suffering and crucifixion. If Paul is victorious, it will not be through his theological supremacy but only because God has reversed his defeats, as God did the death of Christ. Again, a portrayal of Paul as one who triumphed over his theological enemies is not the one that emerges from Paul's own letters.

To be sure, Paul expected to gain the crown of glory, but only because he was faithful, not because he gained theological victories over his opponents. Paul therefore meant it seriously when he affirmed all was of grace, nothing of works, and we do him no credit to assume his theological victories over his opponents cast his life in contradiction to his theology. The portrayal of Paul we have seen in these pages is therefore consonant not only with the evidence we have found about what he said of his life but also with what he said in his theology. One must wonder if any other kind of portrait of Paul will do justice to the one who at the last admitted to the Corinthians that his mission to them bore the marks of failure (2 Cor. 13:7). If there was to be victory, it would be because of the grace and power of God working through Christ, not because Paul was able to carry the day by scoring one theological victory after another. Even such "confidence in the flesh" (Phil. 3:3) was denied to Paul.[7] His confidence was in Christ, and it remained there, even though to outward appearances, he was defeated and wasting away. Defeated in things that were "seen," Paul's confidence rested in things that were "unseen" (2 Cor. 4:18). To understand him in any other way is to continue the victory of Paul's opponents and to continue to obscure the basis in grace of the message of renewal and hope he sought to bring to the people of his day.

Appendix 1

THE APOSTOLIC DECREE

There has been a lively debate over the years about many aspects of the "Apostolic Decree," to which we can here only point. The debate is prompted by the internal evidence in Acts, since there are three accounts of the content of the decrees, two of which (15:29 and 21:25) agree ("things sacrificed to idols [*eidōlothyton*], blood, what is strangled and unchastity") against the third (15:20, "pollutions of idols [*alisgēmata ton eidōlōn*], unchastity, what is strangled and blood"). In addition, the textual traditions show a variety of differences, an indication that early on there was lack of understanding about the intention, and even the content, of these decrees.[1] Codex Bezae (D), for example, omits the reference to strangled things, and replaces it with a form of the golden rule.[2] That change was very likely prompted by the ambiguity attached to such a word as *aima*, particularly in conjunction with *pniktos*. If the reference to blood is a prohibition against eating it, then it and the reference to strangled things constitute only one prohibition,[3] namely, eating flesh with the blood still in it, something forbidden alike to Jews and to the Gentiles resident among them (e.g., Lev. 17:10). If on the other hand, the reference to blood is to be construed as a prohibition against murder, then it becomes a fourth prohibition, different from the command to abstain from eating the flesh of strangled animals.[4]

Such reflections on the textual variants have prompted the suggestion that the original decree underlying the narrative in Acts contained only three prohibitions (either *porneias*[5] or *tou pniktou*[6] was absent), or perhaps only two (those pertaining to blood and to idolatry[7]). A similar lack of clarity has prevailed with respect to the word *porneia*. Suggestions have varied with respect to its meaning in this context: that it means sexual misconduct generally, hence "fornication";[8] that it cannot mean "fornication";[9] that it refers to ritual harlotry;[10] to adultery;[11] to mixed marriages that lead to idolatry;[12] to degrees of consanguinity in marriage forbidden to Jews and hence equal to incest;[13] that it cannot mean such degrees of consanguinity;[14] or that it refers to any sexual activity forbidden in the Jewish law.[15]

Two issues stand paramount, and finally underlie all of the aspects embraced in this discussion: the origin of the prohibitions contained in the decree, and, hence, their intent, whether moral or ritual. While there is some inclination to attribute these decrees to a summary of the "Noachian commands," six of which according to rabbinic tradition had been given by God to Adam at the time of creation (prohibitions against worshiping other gods, blasphemy of God's name, cursing judges, murder, incest and adultery, and robbery), and again to Noah, with a seventh added (prohibition of eating blood), it is difficult to justify the reduction of the six or seven to four, since all were thought to have universal validity.[16] As a result, derivation of the decree from those commands has seemed somewhat unlikely. More support has been given the notion that they derive from the commands listed in Leviticus 17—19, where all elements found in the Apostolic Decree are discussed, and in a context that includes mention of all who live in Israel, Israelites and sojourners (foreigners) alike.[17] The problem again, however, lies in the fact that while the four elements are discussed, so are many others, and only three commands are explicitly addressed to sojourners as well as Israelites (17:8–9, the command that sacrifices must be brought to the door of the tent of meeting; 17:10–16, the prohibition against eating blood; 20:1–5, the prohibition against offering children to Moloch). Only two of those (blood, Moloch) have any reference to elements in the Apostolic Decree (blood, idolatry).

The origin of the commands, uncertain as it is, will therefore not aid in determining if the original intent of the commands was ritual[18] or moral.[19] Again, there are problems with both. If they were intended to set out the minimal ritual conditions under which Jew and Gentile could have table fellowship, the absence of any mention of eating unclean foods, such as pork, is remarkable, especially since this prohibition was widely known even among non-Jews in the Roman Empire to be a regular characteristic of Jewish dietary prescriptions. To argue that it was well known and hence did not require mention could also apply to eating food with the blood in it, or to idolatry, characteristics of Jews equally widely known. In addition, the double mention of eating blood (*aima* and *pnikta*) is difficult to explain.

If, on the other hand, the reference to blood meant murder, and hence the decrees were intended to present a kind of irreducible minimum of ethical behavior required of gentile (and presumably also of Jewish) Christians, one must again wonder at the limitation to four, and question why "strangled things" was included among minimal ethical admonitions. To hold with Thorlief Boman that the original decree, written in Greek, was ethical, but that the Aramaic translation, also made at the Apostolic Council, unintentionally altered it in a cultic direction, is ingenious but probably represents a victory of ingenuity over history.[20] Mandrick Manek is more likely to be correct in accounting for the text-history of the passage when he argues that the transformation into a set of moral instructions (hence the elimination of *pnikta* and the introduction of the golden rule in Codex Bezae [D]) was done by the fathers to eliminate the contradiction between Acts 15 (ritual conditions) and Galatians 2 (no conditions from Jewish side).[21] Moral rules could apply to both Jew and Gentile, and it is obvious from Paul's letters that he would have had no objection to requiring both to observe the kind of elemental moral rules presumed in the Apostolic Decree.

The tendency of the later church to change the rules to reflect moral injunctions probably argues for an earlier ritual cast to the decrees. That would be particularly true if the issue was church unity and the crux was table fellowship, which could then also include participation in a common eucharist. It would also help explain Paul's evident displeasure with the decree, coming, as I have argued it did, after Paul had thought the issue was settled at the meeting he described in Gal. 2:1–10.

Appendix 2

LUKE AND
THE SHAPING OF ACTS 15

If in fact Luke allowed certain assumptions about the way the early church functioned—assumptions he drew almost certainly from his close attention to his sources (see Luke 1:3)[1]—to determine the way he interpreted and presented sources that were fragmentary or uncertain, then there ought to be evidences that he also had a hand in the formulation of the present narrative in Acts 15. Since recent scholarship has concluded that this is precisely the case, it is worth noting some of those conclusions.

One important piece of evidence that Luke has had a hand in shaping this account lies in the fact that when James quotes from Amos 9 in his speech (Acts 15:15–18), the quotation is drawn from the Septuagint (Greek translation of the Old Testament: LXX). Further, James quotes the LXX precisely at a place where it differs significantly from the Hebrew original (the Masoretic text: MT), something one would hardly have expected the historical James to have done.[2] Such explanations as that James was quoting from a Hebrew text at variance with the MT, since the historical situation would not have allowed James to quote any text "at variance with the original Hebrew," is in my view a speculative attempt to rescue the scholar from the rather evident state of affairs.[3]

Again, the central role of the Apostolic Decree in Luke's account of the council in Acts 15, an account with numerous problems, has led many to question whether the Decree in fact had any historical association with the assembly Luke describes there. The decree is not only reported in differing forms within the report of the council (cf. Acts 15:20 with 29), it is also mentioned to Paul at a much later time as though he were learning of it for the first time (21:25). Again, the decree does not address what Luke had identified as the occasion for the council in the first place: the necessity of circumcision for salvation. Thus, whatever view one may take about the origin of the decree (see Appendix 1), its presence as a key conclusion of the council described in Acts 15 creates severe problems for those who want to understand it more as a historical report than as a Lukan construction.[4]

The explicit mention of elders in Jerusalem, who, along with the apostles, served as the group to whom appeal had to be made (Acts 15:2, 4) has also been cited as evidence that raises the question of the extent of Luke's compositional activity.[5] There is, for example, a notable lack of clarity about the composition of that group of elders. It is not clear whether their mention in Acts 15:6, 22–23, refers to the elders permanently resident in Jerusalem, or whether the term in those verses covers all participants other than apostles. To argue with S. J. Gaechter that they came from all participating churches, thus making the assembly in Acts 15 comparable to the kind of council known from later church history, is probably to see the events anachronistically.[6]

Other items, such as the question as to whether Paul was even present at the council which underlies Luke's narrative in Acts 15—the absence of Luke's account of any speech by Paul may be due to the fact there was no record of one because he did not give one, and that he gave none since he was not there[7]—have also led to the question about the historical reliability of even the broader details recorded in Acts 15.[8]

Similarly, the attempt to isolate specific sources upon which Luke based his account of the council described in Acts 15 (with the often unarticulated assumption that such sources would bolster the historical reliability of the information thus accounted for) has found no unanimity of result, or even of agreement on what the indications of underlying sources would be that would allow one to differentiate information thus derived from material Luke himself wrote. Proposals have ranged from the attempt to find *the* pre-Lukan source[9] to the attempt to identify more than one source to which materials could be assigned.[10] None of these proposals has succeeded in convincing a majority of scholars.[11]

Rather, the evidence of Lukan shaping of the narrative in Acts 15 is so overwhelming that many have concluded that the account owes more to Lukan literary and theological themes than to a reworking of one or more historically (more or less) reliable sources.[12] That is not to deny that Luke had some prior information on which he based his account in Acts 15.[13] It is simply to affirm that taken as a whole, the report has no historical value in its present form for determining the course of the early church.

Appendix 3

PAUL AND
THE APOSTOLIC DECREE

There has been considerable debate concerning whether or not Paul knew about the Apostolic Decree mentioned in Acts 15 and 21. If Acts 21:25 is accurate, and Paul learned of the decree only at the end of his career, one would naturally expect no mention of it or its contents in his letters.[1] The absence of any obvious reference to it either in Gal. 2:1–10[2] or in 1 Corinthians 8 and 10, where Paul is discussing precisely the kind of problem dealt with in the decree,[3] has also been cited to show that Paul knew neither it nor its contents.

Others, on the contrary, have argued from the form of the argument in 1 Corinthians 8 and 10 that Paul did know the content of the decree, and was commenting on it there.[4] The most detailed discussion, including a review of scholarly opinions,[5] is that of J. C. Hurd, Jr. Professor Hurd argues that between Paul's "previous letter" to the Corinthian Christians (cf. 1 Cor. 5:9; part of its content, Hurd argues, is found in 2 Cor. 6:14—7:1) Paul learned of, and accepted, the decree. As a result, Paul shaped his discussion in 1 Corinthians 8—10 in its light.

Yet other scholars find evidence that Paul knew the decree from the language of the Galatians 2:6;[6] or from the language of Galatians 5:19–21;[7] or from the language of 2 Corinthians 12:16.[8] I would want to urge that Paul indeed did at some point learn about it, but chose to ignore it,[9] because it may well have represented in his mind an outright denial of the agreement he had reached with James, Peter, and John, an agreement which he certainly would have continued to regard as valid, despite the changes instigated, or at least presided over, by James and accepted by Peter (and Barnabas).

Yet the evidence for determining whether or not Paul knew the decree is ambiguous at best. If certainty is not possible, we can at least form some notion of what was most likely. From Paul's reference to the "contribution to the saints" in 1 Corinthians 16:1–4, it is evident that this passage, and indeed in all likelihood the entire letter, was written after the events Paul described in Gal. 2:1–10, where he agreed to make just such a collection. The same may be said for the passage in 2 Cor. 8:16—9:14 where he also discussed that collection. On the other hand, from the way Paul speaks of Barnabas in 1 Cor. 9:6 ("Or is it only Barnabas and I who have no right to refrain from working for a living?"), we may infer not only that Paul and Barnabas were working together when Paul evangelized Corinth, but also that they were still working together when the letter was written. That is, it would appear that the events described in Gal. 2:11–13 had not yet happened when this passage was written to the Corinthians. If that is the case, then, on our construal of the events, Paul would in fact not yet have known about the decree. It is hard to imagine Paul could have written in so sympathetic a vein of Barnabas, and could have linked Barnabas to himself if Barnabas had already proved himself a "hypocrite" vis-à-vis the true gospel (RSV Gal. 2:13 renders the Greek *hypocritēs* as "insincerity," something of a bowdlerization of the text).

Similarly, it is hard to imagine that Paul could have written about Christian conduct as he did in 1 Cor. 9:19–22 or 10:32 if he had known of the decree, with its treatment of these very topics. In this connection I find unpersuasive the suggestion by Robert G. Hoerber that Paul was silent about the decree in his discussion in 1 Corinthians because the question there concerned the relation between gentile Christians and pagan society, while the decree concerned the imposition of Jewish obligations on gentile Christians. It was precisely the intent of the decree that those Jewish obligations be observed by gentile Christians in *all* their relations, whether with Jews or Gentiles, since those regulations concerned the matter of being a Christian in the first place. Excused from circumcision as part of their life style, gentile Christians were nevertheless, *as Christians* to observe the decree.[10]

Again, that the discussion of "idolatry" and "immortality," contained in 1 Cor. 10:7–8, is due to their inclusion in the decree is doubtful, since the other two members of the quadrad Paul discusses in rhetorically similar terms in this text are "putting the Lord to the test" and "grumbling," items hardly associated in any way with the decree.

On the other hand, that Paul would carry on such discussions with no reference to the decree would argue that if he did know it at that time, he chose to ignore it.

Finally, given the tendentious nature of the narrative in Acts, one ought to be hesitant about attempting to resolve problems such as this on the basis of the order in which the cities are listed which were visited by Paul during the three "missionary journeys" that Acts describes. While Luke surely had traditions that reflected actual events, the order in which he put those traditions owes more to his conception of the way the church developed (his "biases") than to any actual order supposedly contained in those traditions. To argue as some do, therefore, about the correct order of the journeys[11] in Acts strikes one as an exercise in futility.

NOTES

INTRODUCTION

1. A convenient summary of the evidence that tells against such a view as that presented in Acts can be found in Bauer's *Orthodoxy and Heresy in Earliest Christianity*.

2. For such problems in Galatians, see Betz, *Galatians*. For Matthew, see Thompson, *Matthew's Advice to a Divided Community; Mt. 17,22—18,35*. For Mark, see Weeden, *Mark—Traditions in Conflict*. For the Johannine epistles, see Raymond E. Brown, *The Epistles of John*.

CHAPTER 1
THE PROBLEM

1. On this matter, see Bronson, "Paul, Galatians, and Jerusalem," *JAAR* 35 (1967): 123, 125; Betz, *Galatians*, 82.

2. See Bronson, "Paul, Galatians, and Jerusalem," 128; and Mussner, "Die Bedeutung des Apostelkonzils für die Kirche," 45.

3. The term "absolute chronology" refers to a chronology of dates universally applicable to all events, while the term "relative chronology" refers to the specific order in which those events occurred, regardless of whether or not they can be fixed on some absolute chronological line. For a review of some recent works on the problems of both a relative and an absolute chronology for the events in Paul's life in relationship to the accounts in Acts, see Murphy-O'Connor, "Pauline Missions Before the Jerusalem Conference," *RB* 89 (1982): 71–91. The works he reviews are listed on p. 71.

4. Paul also speaks of his intention to make a third visit in Rom. 15:25, but there is no further indication in his letters about whether or not he was able to fulfill that intention.

5. Martyn's *History and Theology in the Fourth Gospel*; Raymond E. Brown's

NOTES

The Church the Apostles Left Behind; and *Community of the Beloved Disciple* are good examples of this genre.

6. E.g., Zuntz, "An Analysis of the Report about the Apostolic Council."

7. Knox, *Chapters in a Life of Paul*.

8. Richard Jeske put it very succinctly: "The proper procedure is to begin with the data from Paul and to utilize the data from Acts, after critical assessment, alongside the Pauline scheme" ("Luke and Paul on the Apostle Paul," [*Cur TM* 4 (1977): 29]). See also Eckert, "Paulus und die Jerusalemer Authoritäten nach des Galaterbriefes und der Apostelgeschichte"; and Zeitlin, "Paul's Journeys to Jerusalem," *JQR* 57 (1966–67): 171–78.

9. See Mussner, "Die Bedeutung," 132; Jack T. Sanders, "Paul's 'Autobiographical' Statements in Galatians 1—2," *JBL* 85 (1966): 335–43.

10. Parker, "Once More, Acts and Galatians," *JBL* 86 (1967): 179.

11. Rudolph Pesch, "Das Jerusalemer Abkommen und die Lösung des Antiochenischen Konflikts," 108–9.

12. Oepke, *Der Brief Paulus an die Galater*, 52.

13. Stein, "The Relationship of Galatians 2:1–10 and Acts 15:1–35: Two Neglected Arguments," *JEvTs* 17 (1974): 239–42.

14. Talbert summarizes the possible views under seven categories in "Again: Paul's Visits to Jerusalem," *NovT* 9 (1967): 26 n. 3.

15. Beck finds three possible modes of viewing the relationship in "The Role of the Jerusalem Conference in the Acts of the Apostles," 3.

16. E.g., Fitzmyer, "The Letter to the Galatians," *JBC*, 239.

17. Knox, *Chapters in a Life of Paul*, 54, pass.

18. Bornkamm affirms in the same locus that careful analysis of the nature of Acts means scholars ought "to abandon the widespread practice of uncritically combining Acts and the letters, and to use great restraint in drawing upon the former" (*Paul*, xxi).

19. Such is the view of Oepke, *Galater*, 52; and Gaechter, "Geschichtliches zum Apostelkonzil," *ZKT* 85 (1963): 340, to cite but two examples.

20. So, e.g., Schlier, *Der Brief an die Galater*, 73.

21. Morton Scott Enslin has used this method (reported by Toussaint, "The Chronological Problem of Galatians 2:1–10," *B Sac* 120 [1963]: 335), and it is also the method favored by Zeitlin, "Paul's Journeys to Jerusalem" *JQR* 57 (1966–67): 171–78.

22. V. Kesich implies that to find conflict within the early church on the basis of comparing Acts and Galatians is "to fit the evidence to our own liking and to our assumptions concerning the developments in the apostolic Church" ("The Apostolic Council at Jerusalem," *St.VTQ* 6 [1962]: 108–17). His method of finding only harmony among the sources is even more obviously open to the charge of fitting evidence to preconceived notions.

23. A good recent summary of the evidence that makes such a conclusion, in my view, inevitable can be found in Mussner, *Der Galaterbrief*, in excursus 2, which begins on p. 128. Such contradiction is enhanced by the impression

93

one gets that Paul in his account in Galatians is seeking to correct false information, as Eckert points out ("Paulus und die Jerusalemer Authoritäten," 284).

24. I will follow the convention that "Luke" is the author of Acts, without in any sense thereby intending to give historic credence to the later traditions about the author; nor do I mean thereby to assert that the author must necessarily have been male. The prominence of women in the early church, e.g., Prisca and Phoebe, means one cannot rule out a priori the possibility that the author of Luke-Acts was a woman.

CHAPTER 2
THE EVIDENCE IN ACTS

1. A visit of Barnabas and "Saul" to Jerusalem is reported in 11:30, but it was concerned with famine relief, not conditions of entry into the Christian community. We will have more to say about this visit below.

2. For a discussion of the problems posed by the content of the decrees, see Appendix 1.

3. E.g., Fischer, "Das Sogennante Apostelkonzil," 14 n. 69; Perrot, "L'Assemblee de Jerusalem," *RSR* 69 (1981): 205; Talbert, "Again: Paul's Visits to Jerusalem," *NovT* 9 (1967): 38.

4. Haenchen, *Die Apostelgeschichte*, 470.

5. So by inference also J. N. Sanders, "Peter and Paul in Acts," *NTS* 2 (1955): 140.

6. Borse, "Kompositionsgeschichtliche Beobachtungen zum Apostelkonzil," 198; Hurd, *The Origin of 1 Corinthians*, 36.

7. As Oepke has suggested in *Der Brief Paulus an die Galater*, 53.

8. So Borse, "Kompositionsgeschichtliche Beobachtungen zum Apostelkonzil," 198–199.

9. See Hurd, *Origin of 1 Corinthians*, 255 n. 4 for a review of such views.

10. Pesch argues that the reference to the speech by Barnabas and Paul appears to be inserted ("eingeschoben") between vv. 12a and 13, especially since James makes no reference to it, and suggests that this may indicate Paul and Barnabas were not there, and that James's speech was part of a pre-Lukan tradition originally referring to the incident with Cornelius ("Das Jerusalemer Abkommen und die Lösung des Antiochenischen Konflikts," 118).

11. J. N. Sanders argues that the absence of the speech itself is due to Luke's lack of any record of such a speech, again since Barnabas and Paul were not there to make one. For other scholars who argue Paul was not present when the decree was formulated, see Nickle, *The Collection: A Study in Paul's Strategy*, 54–55 n. 39.

12. E.g., Elliott, "Κηφᾶς: Σίμων Πέτρος: ὁ Πέτρος: An Examination of New Testament Usage," *NovT* 14 (1972): 248. Pesch finds in this Aramaic name a further indication of pre-Lukan tradition being employed in the report of the council ("Das Jerusalemer Abkommen," 119).

13. Smothers, "Chrysostom and Symeon (Acts xv, 14)," *HTR* 46 (1953): 203–15, pass.

14. As Smothers shows, there is no unanimity among scholars that the "Symeon" must be Simon Peter; see also Dillon and Fitzmyer, "Acts of the Apostles," *JBC*, 195.

15. Nickle suggests that Acts 15:36–38 reflects a "distorted echo" of the conflict Paul reports in Gal. 2:11–14 (Acts 15:1–3 is another "indefinite trace" of it, *Collection*, 54), but he does not draw any conclusion from that suggestion. We will have more to say about that parallel below.

16. In *The Lives of the Caesars*, Suetonius' reference to a scarcity of food due to prolonged drought concerns only its impact on the city of Rome (*The Deified Claudius* 17.2—19). See Hengel, *Acts and the History of Earliest Christianity*, 111; Strecker, "Die sogennante zweite Jerusalemsreise des Paulus," *ZNW* 53 (1962): 72 n. 39. On this whole question, see Funk, "The Enigma of the Famine Visit," *JBL* 75 (1956): 130–36, pass.

17. Hengel, *Acts and the History of Earliest Christianity*, 118–19.

18. Nickle, *Collection*, 59.

19. Toussaint, "The Chronological Problem of Galatians 2:1–10," *B Sac* 120 (1963), 337.

20. Knox, *Chapters in a Life of Paul*, 72.

CHAPTER 3
THE EVIDENCE IN PAUL

1. Dunn makes this point convincingly in "The Relationship between Paul and Jerusalem according to Galatians 1 and 2," *NTS* 28 (1982): 462–63.

2. Periods of days were reckoned inclusively among the peoples of the Hellenistic world. Thus, by our reckoning, the "after three years" of 1:18 would be two years after Paul's conversion, since Paul would have included the year in which the conversion occurred in those three years. Similarly, the "fifteen days" of that same verse would be counted by us as two weeks, since the day of arrival would constitute the first day of Paul's reckoning, and the day of leaving the last. Compare the German *Heute in acht Tagen* (lit., "today in eight days"), which means "a week from today."

3. For a good discussion of the meaning of this Greek verb, particularly in contrast to *idein* ("to see"), see Dunn, "Relationship between Paul and Jerusalem," 463–65.

4. The phrase was used by Raymond E. Brown in a private discussion on this passage.

5. For an interesting proposal that the three pillar apostles derived their authority from their analogy to the three pillars upon whom God "established the world," namely, the patriarchs, see Aus, "Three Pillars and Three Patriarchs: A Proposal Concerning Gal. 2:9," *ZNW* 70 (1979): 254–61.

6. So also, e.g., Holtz, "Die Bedeutung des Apostelkonzils für Paulus," *NovT* 16 (1974): 126, 142–45.

7. See also Dunn, "Relationship between Paul and Jerusalem," 467–68. Dunn has further pointed out in "The Incident at Antioch" how Paul's language in Galatians 1—2 implies that up to the time of the incident at Antioch (Gal. 2:11–14) Paul had taken for granted the primacy and authority of the Jerusalem church (*JSNT* 18 [1983]: 6).

8. Hengel, *Acts and the History of Earliest Christianity*, 114.

9. E.g., Oscar Cullmann, as reported in Elliott, "Κηφᾶς" 250; cf. Günter Klein, "Galater 2,6–9 und die Geschichte der Jerusalemer Urgemeinde," *ZTK* 57 (1960): 283–84; Fischer finds the hypothesis "bestechend" ("Das Sogennante Apostelkonzil," 6) and Bruce thinks it "plausible" ("Further Thoughts on Paul's Autobiography," 27). Kilpatrick finds a parallel to such a procedure (i.e., Paul's using notes [but not official "minutes"] taken at events to discuss them later) in 1 Cor. 11:23–25 ("Peter, Jerusalem and Galatians 1:13—2:14," *NovT* 25 [1983]: 325).

10. E.g., Fuerst, reported in Fung, "A Note on Galatians 2:3–8," *JEvTS* 25 (1982): 51.

11. Acts 12:17c ("Then he departed to another place") may be a reflection of this change, although as Paul reports it, Peter was obviously still present in Jerusalem at the time of this conference.

12. As Hurd points out, Paul's specific disclaimer that the apostles in Jerusalem added *nothing* to his gospel implies that his opponents had been claiming that *something* had indeed been added (*The Origin of 1 Corinthians*, 268)!

13. The identity of "the poor" remains open; scholarly opinion has ranged from those who hold "poor" to mean those who were economically poor, and not the Jerusalem Christians as such (e.g., Oepke, *Der Brief Paulus an die Galater*, 54), to those who hold it to mean specifically the Jerusalem Christians, not those who were economically poor (e.g., Hengel, *Acts*, 118). Their identity is not significant for our discussion.

14. Hall, "St. Paul and Famine Relief: A Study in Galatians 2:10," *Exp Tim* 82 (1970–71): 310. I think this point improbable.

15. E.g., Fahy, "The Council of Jerusalem," *ITQ* 30 (1963): 238, 240, 242; J. N. Sanders, "Peter and Paul in Acts," *NTS* 2 (1955): 139; Hoerber, "Galatians 2:1–10 and the Acts of the Apostles," *CTM* 31 (1960): 482–91, implies that Titus was in fact circumcised, but thinks it could have occurred after either the conference of Acts 15 or the one described in Gal. 2:1–10.

16. So also Fitzmyer, *The Gospel According to Luke (I–IX)*, 239, who nevertheless acknowledges the ambivalence of the language; for outright rejection of the possibility, see Baur, *Paul, Apostle of Jesus Christ*, 122–23 n. 1; Dunn, "Relationship between Paul and Jerusalem," 469.

17. Although some scholars are adamant in their denial that Paul had ever heard of the decree (e.g., C. K. Barrett, "Apostles in Council and in Conflict," *Aus BR* 31, [1983]: 24), some have argued that Paul reflects an aware-

ness of it in other places, such as his discussion in 1 Corinthians (e.g., Hurd, *Origin of 1 Corinthians*, pass.; Perrot, "L'Assemblée de Jérusalem," *RSR* 69 [1981]: 207). In this instance, I think Barrett has the better of the argument.

18. I question Dunn's assertion that while Peter's apostleship was confirmed in Gal. 2:8, Paul's was not ("Relationship between Paul and Jerusalem," 473). The parallelism of the language of vv. 8a and 8b, where in his usual elliptical style Paul omits the second reference to apostleship, clearly implies the equality of Paul with Peter in their divine authority, a parallelism also found in v. 7 and repeated at the end of v. 9. Paul is explicit that the only difference between them was that he was to "remember the poor."

19. The notion that they had come without James's knowledge or without his sanction is a misguided attempt to preserve the appearance of unity at this point in the life of the church. It is clear in Paul's account that while their relationship to James is not the issue, Paul does not raise any question about their authority. That authority was indeed great enough to sway even Peter and Barnabas; it is difficult to imagine someone other than James with that authority in Jerusalem at this time.

20. If *tōn hagiōn tōn en ierousalem* in v. 26 is a partitive genitive ("among the saints in Jerusalem"), as the RSV understands it, then the gift is for the economically poor among the members of that congregation. If it is an epexigetic genitive ("namely, the saints who are in Jerusalem"), then "poor" is the name for Jerusalem Christians. On the other two occasions in this immediate context where Paul mentions the recipients, he calls them simply "the saints" (15:25, 31). This is of little help, since the service of the offering is to the Jerusalem church as a whole (v. 25), which will accept or reject the offering (v. 3), so "the poor who are in Jerusalem" may be either those in the church who need the gift most, or the term may be another way (as "saints") of identifying the whole church as the recipient. Despite the ambiguity, I would incline to see the phrase as partitive genitive.

CHAPTER 4

THE NATURE OF OUR EVIDENCE

1. It has sometimes been assumed that the autobiographical form of Galatians 1—2 would argue for its objectivity. Yet that form served a variety of purposes in the ancient world, and is to be assessed on its rhetorical rather than its historical function. For a good discussion of this matter, see Lyons, *Pauline Autobiography: Toward a New Understanding*.

2. Barrett, "Apostles in Council and in Conflict," *Aus BR* 31 (1983): 14. Barrett also argues for the one-sided nature of the information Luke possessed about the council he depicts in Acts 15 (ibid., 17). See further Burchard, "Paulus in der Apostelgeschichte," *TLZ* 100 (1975): 882–96, a review of three major commentaries, all of which agree that Luke uses and reworks traditions and other information he had come upon; Marshall, "Recent Study of the

Acts of the Apostles," *Exp Tim* 80, (1968–69): 292–96, is another review with similar conclusions. Weiser, "Das 'Apostelkonzil' (Apg 15,1–35)," *BZ*, NF 28 (1984): 145–67, also locates historical material in Acts in terms of traditions rather than specific written sources.

3. Though most scholars would argue that Luke did not have, or even know of, Paul's letters (e.g., J. N. Sanders, "Peter and Paul in Acts," *NTS* 2 [1955]: 143), Enslin, "Once Again, Luke and Paul," *ZNW* 61 (1970): 253–71, argued that Luke had known them, although he misunderstood much and quoted nothing. Enslin's arguments remain unconvincing: While he cites Luke's reworking of Mark and Matthew as evidence of his way of using sources (255–56), he also argues that Luke reworked Paul's letters in a very different way (268), thus destroying the effect of the analogy he proposed. He also argues that when words from Paul's letters turn up in Acts, it shows Acts' dependence (262), while dissimilar wording also shows the use of those same sources (263); it is as hard to refute an argument that appeals to both sides for support as it is to be persuaded by it.

4. J. N. Sanders, "Peter and Paul in Acts," 143.

5. Bronson, "Paul, Galatians, and Jerusalem," *JAAR* 35 (1967): 119.

6. Those who find that Galatians 2 and Acts 15 describe the same conference will argue that Luke knew of only one such conference; e.g., Barrett, "Apostles in Council and in Conflict," 22, 26.

7. E.g., Nickle, *The Collection: A Study in Paul's Strategy*, 53.

8. E.g., Haenchen, *Die Apostelgeschichte*, 456, reporting on Spitta.

9. E.g., Zuntz, "An Analysis of the Report about the Apostolic Council"; Dillon and Fitzmyer, "Acts of the Apostles," *JBC*, 195, but with caveats.

10. E.g., Strecker, "Die sogennante zweite Jerusalemsreise des Paulus," *ZNW* 53 (1962): 69; John Hurd believes the whole account is a literary creation of the author of Acts (*The Origin of 1 Corinthians*, 40–41).

11. E.g., Pesch, "Das Jerusalemer Abkommen und die Lösung des Antiochenischen Konflikts," 121–22; cf. also Conzelmann, *Die Apostelgeschichte*, 87.

12. Schlier holds it as possible that they were not formulated there (*Der Brief an die Galater*, 77); Hurd regards it as certain that they were not (*Origin of 1 Corinthians*, 253). Hengel, *Acts and the History of Earliest Christianity*, 117, and Mussner, *Der Galaterbrief*, 130, argue that they were formulated at a later point than the council recorded in Acts 15.

13. E.g., Conzelmann, *Die Apostelgeschichte*, 85; Haenchen, *Die Apostelgeschichte*, 468; Krodel, *Acts*, 96. Not all agree, however; see Schlier, *Der Brief an die Galater*, 77, who finds an indication of them in Gal. 2:6.

14. The general assumption is that this was the Semitic form of "Simon," i.e., Peter (e.g., Elliott, "Κηφᾶς" *Nov T* 14 [1972]: 248). Weiser argues that this is an example of deliberate archaizing on the part of Luke to give the impression of originality to the report ("Das 'Apostelkonzil' [Apg. 15,1–35]," *BZ*, NF28 [1984]: 154).

15. Some scholars connect Acts 15:39 directly to Gal. 2:11–13 (e.g., Holtz, "Die Bedeutung des Apostelkonzils für Paulus," *NovT* [1974]: 113); others find only an echo of Galatians 2 in Acts 15 because of the different reasons given for the split: in Acts, a dispute about John Mark accompanying Paul and Barnabas on missionary travels; in Galatians a dispute about the place of legal restrictions in the life of a Christian (e.g., Nickle, *Collection*). Hengel thought Luke "knew about the deeper reasons . . . but deliberately kept quiet about them" (*Acts and the History of Earliest Christianity*, 213). Why an author who did such things should be regarded as reliable is difficult to comprehend.

16. So Barrett, "Apostles in Council and in Conflict," 25. In this connection, the question of Paul's stance vis-à-vis circumcision is complicated even though the apparent demand that Titus be circumcised (Gal. 2:3; so Joseph Hainz, "Gemeinschaft [*koinonia*] zwischen Paulus und Jerusalem [Gal. 2:9f.]," 30–42), perhaps also reflected in Acts 15:5 (so Nickle, *Collection*, 57), was successfully rejected by Paul (Holtz argues that held from then on for all of Paul's missionary career, "Die Bedeutung des Apostelkonzils für Paulus," 119). The report of Paul's opponents that Paul did preach circumcision, implied in Gal. 5:11 (for a summary of the opponents' statements, see Jewett, "The Agitators and the Galatians Congregation" *NTS* 17 [1970–71]: 198–212), would have found support in the account of Timothy's circumcision in Acts 16:1–4 (so Talbert, "Again: Paul's Visits to Jerusalem," *NovT* 9 [1967]: 33). While the account in Acts 16 surely fits Luke's desire to show that Paul was not opposed to the law (Borse, "Kompositionsgeschichtliche Beobachtungen zum Apostelkonzil," 207, although he seems to think it historical, 205 n. 35), the lack of any other basis for the opponents' charges in Gal. 5:11 makes it difficult to discredit outright Luke's account regarding Timothy.

17. On this point, see J. N. Sanders, "Peter and Paul in Acts," *NTS* 2 (1955): 136. Enslin, "Emphases and Silences," *HTR* 73 (1980): 219–225, on the contrary, felt that Luke, with his access to Paul's letters, knew quite clearly about the reason for Paul's last visit to Jerusalem, but chose to suppress it, substituting the story, found in Acts 21:17–26, of the four men whose expenses Paul paid so they could absolve themselves of their vows (p. 224).

18. So John Knox affirmed (e.g., *Chapters in a Life of Paul*, 70–71).

19. On this point, cf. Strecker, "Die sogennante zweite Jerusalemsreise des Paulus," *ZNW* 53 (1962): 73–75; he also discusses the problems involved in the passage in Acts 11:27–30 taken by itself, even without any reference to a later Jerusalem visit with a collection, and concludes that the earlier visit reported in Acts 11 never occurred.

20. For a good discussion of the problems involved in the offerings brought to Jerusalem as reported in Acts, see Funk, "The Enigma of the Famine Visit," *JBL* 75 (1956): pass.

CHAPTER 5
THE SHAPE OF ACTS

1. See Appendix 2 for a discussion of the evidence for the assumption that Luke had a hand in shaping the narrative he presents in Acts 15.

2. Dillon and Fitzmyer summarize them as "(1) the importance of Jerusalem as the mother church, the seat of the Twelve, and the doctrinal focal point of Christian missionary activity; (2) the work of the Spirit in guiding the spread of the Word, in forming the Christian community, and in bringing men into the fold" ("Acts of the Apostles," 166 col. 1). For more detailed discussion, one may consult Knox, *Chapters in a Life of Paul*, 25–29, or Haenchen, *Die Apostelgeschichte*, 88–93.

3. Bauernfeind was correct when he described the conference reported in Acts 15 as "*one* great scene, where the leaders act in the presence of the assembled congregation" (quoted in Haenchen, *Die Apostelgeschichte*, 457). Weiser also emphasized the importance for Luke not only that the whole community be present at the council, but that everything be done with unanimity (*homothymadon*, v. 25), one of Luke's central concerns ("Das 'Apostelkonzil' [Apg. 15:1–35]," *BZ*, NF 28 [1984]: 163, 165).

4. Scribal copyists found no problem with the presence of this name; it stands in Acts 15:14 without variant (see Elliott, "Κηφᾶς," *Nov T* 14 [1972]: 248).

5. Zuntz also concludes that the presence of Paul and Barnabas is due to Lukan authorial activity ("An Analysis of . . . the Apostolic Council," 238).

6. See Beck, "The Role of the Jerusalem Conference in the Acts of the Apostles," 134. Alfons Weiser argues that the inclusion of Silas, a leading figure from Jerusalem, as one of those who carried the decree to the gentile churches also represents Luke's attempt to show that Paul's further work as missionary among the Gentiles met with the approval of the Jerusalem authorities ("Das 'Apostelkonzil,'" 164).

7. Weiser, "Das 'Apostelkonzil,'" 165; Hengel, *Acts and the History of Earliest Christianity*, 115. Mussner sees the later beginning of "heretical Jewish Christianity" as evidence that such harmony did not exist ("Die Bedeutung des Apostelkonzils für die Kirche," 45). Paul's continued opposition to any required observance of the law points in the same direction (e.g., Gal. 2:19, 21; 3:2–3, 5).

8. That the question would in fact not rest is clear from Paul's discussion in Galatians, esp. chap. 5. Jewett ("The Agitators and the Galatians Congregation," *NTS* 17 [1970–71]: 209) also points to Gal. 1:6 and 3:1–5 as showing that the problem was far from being resolved, and Lyons (*Pauline Autobiography: Toward a New Understanding*, 127) argues that the Galatians awaited only Paul's permission to undergo circumcision themselves.

9. It was precisely that decree, as we shall argue below, which brought about the conflict between Peter and Barnabas on the one hand, and Paul on

the other, a conflict reported in Gal. 2:11–14 and underlying Acts 15:36–40.

10. It is possible that the account of the dispute between Paul and Barnabas about John Mark was part of the tradition about the latter's forsaking the mission Luke reports in Acts 13:13b, but that Luke detached it in order to account for the tradition he also had of a dispute between the two chief missionaries to the Gentiles following the Apostolic Council and the Apostolic Decree. That more than one such argument occurred is on the face of it likely, and thus Luke's having two traditions of dispute would not be surprising. There is as little likelihood that the gentile missionary movement unrolled without dispute as there is that the entire mission of the church proceeded in that way; Acts itself contains enough evidence to make both assumptions gratuitous.

11. Strecker concluded that the journey Luke reports in Acts 11:27–30 never occurred ("Die Sogennante zweite Jerusalemsreise des Paulus," *ZNW* 53 [1962]: 75), a judgment I would be inclined to support; Knox implies the same conclusion (*Chapters in a Life of Paul*, 69–72).

12. For an irenic explanation of how the two accounts could arise without malice or intentional deceit on either side, see Cambier, "Le Voyage de S. Paul a Jerusalem en Act. ix.26ss. et la Schema Missionnaire Theologique de s. Luc," *NTS* 8 (1962): 255–56. I believe that in broad outline he is correct in his understanding of the situation that produced the two accounts.

13. For example, that the Apostolic Decree was not formulated at the council in Jerusalem where Paul was present, since Paul did not learn of that decree until later: Gal. 2:10; Acts 21:25; that there was a mission-rending split between Barnabas and Paul after the Apostolic Decree was formulated: Gal. 2:11–14; Acts 15:37–40; that Paul's reason for the journey to Jerusalem that resulted in his arrest was the bringing of an offering: Rom. 15:25, cf. v. 31; Acts 24:17.

CHAPTER 6
THE EVENTS UNDERLYING ACTS AND GALATIANS

1. Several scholars have sought to solve the problem of the visits reported in Acts 11 and 15 by arguing that they really report the same event; so, e.g., Catchpole, "Paul, James and the Apostolic Decree," *NTS* 23 (1977): 436; Duncan, *The Epistle of Paul to the Galatians*, xxiv–xxv; Nickle, *The Collection: A Study in Paul's Strategy*, 53; Pesch, "Das Jerusalemer Abkommen und die Lösung des Antiochenischen Konflikts," 110–11; for objections to that identification, see Parker, "Once More, Acts and Galatians," *JBL* 86 (1967): 178–79. Funk, on the other hand, has argued that the famine visit and Paul's final visit to Jerusalem are the same, "The Enigma of the Famine Visit," *JBL* 75 (1956): 131, 132, 136.

2. There is also the theoretical possibility that a tradition reflecting a Lukan presupposition would agree with a tradition found in Paul. Yet in that case, by definition, the tradition in Acts would not reflect a Lukan bias, precisely

because it appears also in Paul. That remains, however, a purely theoretical possibility, since no tradition displaying such agreement has been identified.

3. In this instance there is the added point that the "great famine over all the world" during the reign of Claudius to which Luke refers in Acts 11:28 is otherwise unattested in ancient sources; see chap. 2 n. 16.

4. An equation between Acts 9:26–30 and Gal. 1:18–24 has also been suggested by Hoerber, "Galatians 2:1–10 and the Acts of the Apostles," *CTM* 31 (1960): 483; Kesich also implies that identification, "The Apostolic Council at Jerusalem, *St. VTQ* 6 (1962): 109. See also, on this point, Hemer, "Acts and Galatians Reconsidered," *Themelios* 2 (1977): 87, where he is following Bruce, "Further Thoughts on Paul's Autobiography," 81. Hemer then equates Gal. 2:1–10 with Acts 11:27–30, a point we will argue against. See also Talbert, "Again: Paul's Visits to Jerusalem," *NovT* 9 (1967): 35. On the other hand, Parker, ("Once More, Acts and Galatians," 180) argued that Acts 9:26–30 was due entirely to the compositional activity of Luke, and that this account therefore bears no relationship to historical reality.

5. For examples of arguments brought forward to defend the thesis that the visit to Jerusalem and the ensuing meeting reported in Gal. 2:1–10 are to be equated with the visit to Jerusalem recorded as the "famine visit" of Acts 11:27–30, see Duncan, *Epistle of Paul to the Galatians*, xxii–xxiii; Catchpole, "Paul, James and the Apostolic Decree," 432–44; Toussaint, "The Chronological Problems of Galatians 2:1–10," *B Sac* 120 (1963): 338–39. For objections to such an equation, see Fischer, "Das Sogennante Apostelkonzil," 10–22, n. 46; Hall, "St. Paul and Famine Relief: A Study in Galatians 2:10," *Exp Tim* 82 (1970–71): 310; Strecker, "Die Sogennante zweite Jerusalemsreise des Paulus," *ZNW* 53 (1962): 68–69, 75. The identification of Galatians 2 with Acts 15 also continues to find occasional support; e.g., Stein, "The Relationship of Galatians 2:1–10 and Acts 15:1–35: Two Neglected Arguments," *JEvTS* 17 (1974): 241–42; Zeitlin, "Paul's Journeys to Jerusalem," *JQR* 57 (1966–67): 176. Good summaries of the various positions scholars have taken on this question can be found in the articles by Hemer, "Acts and Galatians Reconsidered," and Stein, "Relationship of Galatians 2:1–10 and Acts 15:1–35."

6. In some Western texts the "not . . . to them ("we did *not* yield *to them*," Gal. 2:5) is absent, but even though the omission is clearly the *lexio difficilior* at least as far as context is concerned, it is hard to see how that omission could be original; cf. Wolfe, "A New Path: How a Textual Variant Provides Additional Insight, *CM*, Jan. 1979, 19.

7. Some Western texts replace "Cephas" with "Peter" and reverse the order of James and Peter in Gal. 2:9, so that the list begins with "Peter"; on this see Elliott, "Κηφᾶς," *Nov T* 14 (1979): 249. J. N. Sanders, "Peter and Paul in Acts," *NTS* 2 (1955): 137, suggests that if Paul did in fact list Peter first, it was because the James to whom he referred in that account was the not Lord's brother but rather the Son of Zebedee.

NOTES

8. While it has been argued that this order shows a change in leadership from the time of Gal. 1:18–19 (e.g., Fung, "A Note on Galatians 2:3–8," *JEvTS* 25 [1982]: 51), Klein argues that the transfer had not even taken place by the time of Gal. 2:1–10 ("Galater 2,6–9 und die Geschichte der Jerusalemer Urgemeinde," *ZTK* 57 [1960]: 290). One must be careful not to argue for the sole authority of Peter in Gal. 1:18–19, however, as Klein does on the basis of the "nonchalant addition" of James in v. 19, since that "nonchalant" mention indicates that even at that time, one could not visit Jerusalem without due deference to James. To argue as Salvatore Alberto Panimolle does in "L'Autorité de Pierre en *Ga* 1—2 et *AC* 15," that Paul's visit to Peter in these verses demonstrates already at that time the primacy of Peter, I find unfounded.

9. Haenchen argues that on the basis of the mention of Antioch in Gal. 2:11, we are to infer that Paul and Barnabas went to Jerusalem as representatives of the Antioch church in the visit described in 2:1–10 (*Die Apostelgeschichte*, 464). It may well be that this point is cloaked in Paul's phrase "by revelation," that is, as mediated by that church; his emphasis in the Galatians account on his independence from the Jerusalem authorities for his call to be a missionary might also have led him to omit reference to the fact that he and Barnabas attended the meeting as representatives of the Christian community at Antioch.

10. It is not clear whether or not Paul agreed to two (independent) missions, one to Gentiles without circumcision, the other to Jews with circumcision (so already Baur, *Paul, Apostle of Jesus Christ*, 125). Paul, intent as he was on having the legitimacy of a law-free mission acknowledged, may not have understood a two-mission agreement as the outcome of the conference, and that in turn may help explain his strong reaction to the events in Antioch he described in Gal. 2:11–14.

11. If Paul's language in 2:10 means that he agreed to continue to remember the poor (e.g., Hall, "St. Paul and Famine Relief: A Study in Galatians 2:10," *Exp Tim* 82 (1970–71): 310), it would be in accord with Luke's report of an early offering visit in Acts 11:27–30; if it means he was being asked to do that for the first time (e.g., Knox, *Chapters in a Life of Paul*, 55–57), then Acts 11 drops from view. The grammatical case for the former position appears less persuasive than for the latter.

12. The visit to Jerusalem mentioned in Acts 11:27–30 should, in my view, drop from sight in any discussion of historic events concerning Paul's concourse with Jerusalem; given the mention of that offering in Acts 24:17, which goes against Luke's presuppositions but supports Paul's planned travel (Rom. 15:25), it seems apparent that Acts 11:27–30 owes more to Luke's authorial activity than to any historical traditions. Given Luke's presuppositions, and his (questionable) information about a worldwide famine in the time of Claudius, I would argue that Luke, misunderstanding the tradition about the offering, mislocated it. See also nn. 1, 5, 11 of this chapter.

13. That the Apostolic Decree is to be separated not only from the conference described in Gal. 2:1–10 but also from the one recorded in Acts 15:1–29

103

with the participants Luke listed as in attendance has frequently been argued. For typical arguments, see Hurd, *The Origin of 1 Corinthians*, 255, esp. n. 49; Strobel, "Das Aposteldekret als Folge des Antiochenischen Streites," 60, 82; cf. also Dillon and Fitzmyer, "Acts of the Apostles," 195; Fahy, "The Council of Jerusalem," *ITQ* 30 (1963): 252; Zuntz, "An Analysis of the Report about the Apostolic Council," 290–91.

14. Again, it would have been Luke's assumption that such an important matter would have to have been reached with all interested parties present, if harmony was to be maintained, which led him to assume Paul and Peter would have been present at that conference. Luke knew a tradition that presumed Paul was not present (Acts 21:25), but he chose to ignore its implications.

15. An echo of that split is preserved in Acts 15:39–40, where it also occurred following the conference at which the Apostolic Decree was formulated and sent out.

16. On James assuming leadership, see Klein, "Galater 2,6–9," 290–91; J. N. Sanders, "Peter and Paul in Acts," 137. There may be evidence of certain rivalries concerning leadership in the early church in both canonical and non-canonical evidence. For example, some have argued that the authority of Peter is stressed to such a degree in Matt. 16:18 that a polemic against the claims of another, either James in Jerusalem, or Paul's implied claim to authority over Peter in Gal. 2:11–14, underlies the formulation. Again, the *Apocryphon of James* (15:18–20; 16:8–9) emphasizes the authority of James, perhaps in a polemic against Peter. For a thorough discussion of this topic, see Smith, *Petrine Controversies in Early Christianity*.

17. In light of such evidence, and Luke's conviction, reflected throughout the remainder of Acts, that harmony reigned after the Apostolic Council, one must wonder if the objections to Paul's mission credited by Luke to the "Jews" may not in fact reflect opposition by Jewish *Christians*.

18. I owe this suggestion to Joseph A. Fitzmyer in private discussion; see also Dillon and Fitzmyer, "Acts of the Apostles," 195. Smothers, "Chrysostom and Symeon (Acts xv, 14)," *HTR* 46 (1953): 212–14, reports on an article by Stanislas Giet in which the latter also suggested that the Symeon of Acts 15:14 was in fact Symeon Niger of Acts 13:1 ("L'Assemblée Apostolique et le Décret de Jérusalem. Qui était Syméon?" [*Mélanges Jules Lebreton I* (Paris, 1951) = *RSR* XXXIX, pp. 203ff.]); I have not been able to secure Giet's article.

19. On this understanding neither Peter (cf. Baur, *Paul, Apostle of Jesus Christ*, 128; Simon, "The Apostolic Decree and Its Setting in the Ancient Church," *BJRL* 52 [1952]: 452) nor Paul (e.g., Fahy, "The Council of Jerusalem," *ITQ* 30 [1963]: 244; J. N. Sanders, "Peter and Paul in Acts," *NTS* 2 [1955]: 141; Strobel, "Das Aposteldekret in Galatien: zur Situation von Gal. I and II," *NTS* 20 [1974]: 181; Talbert, "Again: Paul's Visits to Jerusalem," *NovT* 9 [1967]: 35) were present at this second conference. Such a view is of

course intolerable to those who find in Acts 15 evidence of Petrine primacy (e.g., Gaechter, "Geschichtliches zum Apostelkonzil," *ZKT* 85 [1963]: 348–50; Mussner, "Die Bedeutung des Apostelkonzils für die Kirche," 41–43).

20. Kesich suggests that James acted in support of the decree "out of expediency and not as a matter of principle," which perhaps says more about Kesich's view of James than it does about James's own motivation ("The Apostolic Council at Jerusalem," *St. VTQ* 6 [1962]: 110).

21. I.e., not at the earlier conference represented by Gal. 2:1–10; much information about this later conference is contained in the account of Acts 15, but Luke has reshaped it to reflect a more universal conclave; the report now looks very much like a combination of the conferences reported in Gal. 2:1–10 (= Acts 11:1–18) and assumed in Gal. 2:12.

22. There is wide agreement that Paul was not present when the decree was formulated (e.g., Catchpole, "Paul, James and the Apostolic Decree," 431; Eckert, "Paulus und die Jerusalemer Authoritäten," 299; Nickle, *Collection*, 55–56; Strobel, "Das Aposteldekret als Folge des Antiochenischen Streites," 94; but cf. Fahy, "Council of Jerusalem," 247); while Acts 21:25 seems to reflect that later origin (so e.g., Borse, "Kompositionsgeschichtliche Beobachtungen zum Apostelkonzil," 197; J. N. Sanders, "Peter and Paul in Acts," 140; Strobel, "Das Aposteldekret als Folge," 101), not all find that verse significant for this problem (e.g., Catchpole, 431).

23. On the question whether or not Paul's letters contain any evidence that Paul knew about the decree mentioned in Acts 15 and 21, see Appendix 3.

24. Acts 15:19–20 (cf. 21:25) accurately reflects James's responsibility for the decree (e.g., Betz, *Galatians*, 108; Krodel, *Acts*, 96; Strobel, "Das Aposteldekret als Folge," 91). Catchpole points out correctly that this withdrawal shows that the demands from James were not obeyed by (some? all?) gentile Christians ("Paul, James and the Apostolic Decree," 441).

25. So also Strobel, "Das Aposteldekret in Galatien," 185.

26. Catchpole suggests that such a changed situation "requires some interval of time" ("Paul, James and the Apostolic Decree," 442).

27. Dunn ("The Incident at Antioch," *JSNT* 18 [1983]: 31) argues against the possibility we are proposing on the ground that neither Peter nor the Jewish believers in Antioch would have succumbed so completely to such a decree from James. However, just that same kind of confidence, when betrayed, caused Paul to react as forcefully, even violently, as he did. Reflecting the apostolic intemperance of Paul's language is the claim both of the *Epistula Apostolorum 2* and Clement of Alexandria (cited in Eusebius, *Church History* 1.12.2) that the "Cephas" Paul rebuked was not the Apostle Peter! (cited in Smith, *Petrine Controversies in Early Christianity*, 210).

28. Hengel (*Acts and the History of Earliest Christianity*, 120–21) suggests that such separation was what James wanted, to keep Jewish Christians from constantly breaking the law of purity. Yet as Perrot points out, purity would also

105

demand abstention from pork and observance of the Sabbath ("L'Assemblée de Jérusalem," *RSR* 69 [1981]: 199; on the last point [Sabbath] see also Barrett, "Apostles in Council and in Conflict," *Aus BR* 31 [1983]: 25). Even Tacitus recognized those two as essential to Jews, along with circumcision and observance of the passover (*Histories* 5.2–5).

29. See also Pesch, "Das Jerusalemer Abkommen," 120. Bruce suggests that some of the intensity derived from Paul's awareness that Peter was acting against his own convictions in this matter, "Further Thoughts on Paul's Autobiography," 28; see also Strobel, "Das Aposteldekret in Galatien," 180; Nesbitt, "What *Did* Become of Peter?" *JBR* 27 (1959):12, citing Cullman.

30. So also Strobel, "Das Aposteldekret in Galatien," 189. Kesich on the other hand assumes that Paul could easily have agreed to the decree, since it would have made common eucharist possible, and "since the Eucharist is the life of the church . . . these laws were acceptable to everyone" ("Apostolic Council at Jerusalem," 112); on such an anachronistic view, Paul could have accepted the decree at any point. Scott, "Parties in the Church of Jerusalem as seen in the Book of Acts," *JEvTS* 8 (1975), assumes that the decree represented the view of the moderate faction in Jerusalem, seeking to effect a compromise that did not offend Jewish scruples (225), a point totally lacking in Paul's report of his conference in Gal. 2:1–10, but possible if the decree was formulated at a later time. Whatever its intention, however, Paul regarded it as unacceptable.

31. Reicke, "Der geschichtliche Hintergrund des Apostelkonzils und der Antiochia-Episode, Gal. 2,1–14," attempted to resolve the difficulty by attributing it to external factors. For a recent study of possible relevant external factors, see Bronson, "Paul, Galatians, and Jerusalem," *JAAR* 35 (1967) 119–28; Dunn, "The Incident at Antioch," 7–27, 32–33; Jewett, "The Agitators and the Galatians Congregations," *NTS* 17 (1970–71): 204–6. Nevertheless, as Eckert notes ("Paulus und die Jerusalemer Authoritäten," 301 n. 84), all such proposals remain speculative; we have no direct sources of information, and hence we simply do not know what pressures would have been felt by the Jerusalem church.

32. If Scott is correct that the decree was "put forward only as guidelines" to aid Christians in racially mixed Christian communities, it would be difficult to see why Paul would not have gladly accepted and integrated the content of the decree into his message as being quite in line with his own understanding of ethics. Obviously, more than "guidelines" were being proposed by those "men from James."

33. Scott also admits that the "Pharisaic Hebrew Christians" must have regarded the Jerusalem Council that produced the decree as a defeat, and that the continuing problem Paul had with Judaizing influences, and with those who attacked his gospel, probably came from that same group in Jerusalem ("Parties in the Church of Jerusalem," 223). See also Jewett, "Agitators and the Galatians Congregations," 200, 206).

34. Luke will have understood the Jerusalem conference and the decree as further evidence of the fulfillment of Judaism by Christianity (the decree) without its being simply a part of Judaism (no circumcision), and the agreement of both factions to its outcome as further evidence of the harmony of the early church; so also Beck, "The Role of the Jerusalem Conference in the Acts of the Apostles," 338; Manek, "Das Aposteldekret im Kontext," *CV* 15 (1972): 156, 158–59.

CHAPTER 7
SOME HISTORICAL CONCLUSIONS

1. So Barrett, "Apostles in Council and in Conflict," *Aus BR* 31 (1983): 25; Dunn, "The Incident at Antioch," *JSNT* 18 (1983): 31; Hoerber, "The Decree of Claudius in Acts 18:2," *CTM* 31 (1960): 484, 485, 488; Holtz, "Die Bedeutung des Apostelkonzils für Paulus," *NovT* (1974): 124; Kesich, "The Apostolic Council at Jerusalem," *St. VTQ* 6 (1962): 109; Krodel, *Acts*, 96; Nickle, *The Collection: A Study in Paul's Strategy*, 106–7; J. N. Sanders, "Peter and Paul in Acts," *NTS* 2 (1955): 141; Strobel, "Das Aposteldekret in Galatien; zur Situation von Gal. I und II," *NTS* 20 (1974): 188; Toussaint, "The Chronological Problem of Galatians 2:1–10," *B Sac* 120 (1963): 338. Murphy-O'Connor criticizes Luedemann for holding this view, agrees with Jewett who opposes it, but does not develop the point ("Pauline Missions Before the Jerusalem Conference," *RB* 89 [1982]: 81 n. 14).

2. Strobel, "Das Aposteldekret als Folge des Antiochenischen Streites" as a typical example, argues that the tone of the decree is one of understanding, reconciliation, and compromise, which maintained harmony in the church (98). Barrett, on a mildly contrary note, argues that the Jerusalem Conference was a failure, "yet . . . not wholly a failure" ("Apostles in Council and in Conflict," 29).

3. Oepke finds "das überwiegende geschichtliche und sachliche Recht . . . auf seitens des Paulus . . . ," (*Der Brief Paulus an die Galater*, 65); Filson concludes that however the decree be interpreted, "Paul won an immense victory" ("Live Issues in the Acts," 35).

4. On this question, see Appendix 3.

5. Knox senses in Rom. 15:23 ("But now, since I no longer have any room for work in these regions, and since I have longed for many years to come to you") Paul's "relief and pleasure" that his work in the east now permits him to fulfill his desire to visit Rome (*Chapters in a Life of Paul*, 53). That this admits of a rather different interpretation, see below.

6. Weiser finds in Luke's account of the conference in Jerusalem, especially in Acts 15:3, evidence that the group disputing with Paul was a minority ("nur eine Minderheit"), and that most Christians agreed with Paul ("macht Lukas deutlich, dass . . . die meisten Christen mit der paulinischen Weise der Missionsarbeit einverstanden sind," "Das 'Apostelkonzil' [Apg 15, 1–35],"

BZ, NF 28 [1984]: 158). Whether or not that description reflects reality is another matter altogether.

7. So Mussner: "[Die] Einheit [der Kirche] blieb zunaeschst erhalten" ("Die Bedeutung des Apostelkonzils für die Kirche," 46).

8. That is true whether or not the Jerusalem Conference was the cause of the Antioch dispute, as is shown by those who do not regard the Jerusalem Council as the cause of that dispute, e.g., Barrett, "Apostles in Council and in Conflict," 38; Betz, *Galatians*, 104; Catchpole, "Paul, James and the Apostolic Decree," *NTS* 23 (1977): 440; Eckert, "Paulus und die Jerusalemer Authoritäten nach dem Galaterbrief und der Apostelgeschichte," 302; Holtz, "Die Bedeutung des Apostelkonzils," 125.

9. So Dunn, *Unity and Diversity in the New Testament*, 254; Koester, *Introduction to NT*, 2:107.

10. So also J. N. Sanders, "Peter and Paul in Acts," 141. Weiser argues that Silas could not have been a follower of James, and hence could not have brought the decree. If, however, Luke is correct that Silas was one of those who delivered the letter (Acts 15:27, 32), he may have brought it back as a representative of the gentile Christian mission in Antioch that had also sent representatives to the Jerusalem Council under the leadership of Symeon Niger (see chap. 6 n. 18). On the other hand, if Luke was correct in portraying Silas as one of the Jewish Christians in Jerusalem (Acts 15:25a, 33), Silas changed his mind in Antioch, perhaps as a result of the dispute. In either case, if Luke was correct about listing Silas as Paul's new partner in mission following the dispute with Barnabas (Acts 15:39–40), we may infer that Silas was one of the few who supported Paul in the dispute.

11. The phrase is from Catchpole, "Paul, James and the Apostolic Decree," 444.

12. So Oepke, *Der Brief Paulus an die Galater*, 54. Dunn observes that Paul's first journey in Acts begins and ends in Antioch, and hence is a "missionary journey" ("Incident at Antioch," 39). Subsequent travels see Paul settle in other places—Corinth, Ephesus—for lengthy periods; they thus become his base of operations. This probably again reflects Luke's awareness of evidence that did not support his understanding of early Christian history. Is it merely coincidence that Luke calls Paul an "apostle" in connection with that first journey (Acts 14:4, 14), but not in connection with the others?

13. Duncan suggests that they may have followed him from town to town (*The Epistle of Paul to the Galatians*, xxix); see also Enslin, "Emphases and Silences," *HTR* 75 (1980): 221.

14. That the agitators in Galatia were from the same source as those who brought the news from James to Antioch, see Strobel, "Das Aposteldekret als Folge," 84; that those in Corinth were the same, see Dunn, *Unity and Diversity*, 255.

15. So, e.g., Dunn, "Incident at Antioch," 6.

16. So also Dunn, "The Relationship between Paul and Jerusalem according

to Galatians 1 and 2," *NTS* 28 (1982): 471–73; G. Klein, "Galater 2,6–9 und die Geschichte der Jerusalemer Urgemeinde," *ZTK* 57 (1960): 288–89; Betz, *Galatians*, 93, see 93–95 for a survey of other hypotheses. Murphy-O'Connor, "Pauline Missions," on the other hand, has recently defended the idea that it refers to the earlier meeting.

17. Enslin argued that the collection was rejected because it appeared to Paul's Jewish-Christian opponents that he was trying to "buy his way in" ("Once Again, Luke and Paul," *ZNW* 61 [1970]: 270). Ten years later Enslin suggested in the same context that the story of the attempt of Simon the magician to buy the gift of the laying on of hands (Acts 8:9–24) was originally directed against Paul; Luke sought to deflect that charge by making Simon the chief character ("Emphases and Silences," 224–25).

18. So also Dunn, *Unity and Diversity*, 256–57. J. N. Sanders also points out that Luke minimized the conflict and resulting tragedy ("Peter and Paul in Acts," 143).

19. So also Bronson, "Paul, Galatians, and Jerusalem," *JAAR* 35 (1967): 122; Dunn, *Unity and Diversity*, 254.

20. So also Strobel, "Das Aposteldekret in Galatien," 182.

21. Manek notes that Acts represents a compromise between a Jewish Christianity that demanded circumcision of Christians and a Paulinism that denied any validity to the law as a means of salvation ("Das Aposteldekret im Kontext," *CV* 15 [1972]: 159). That "compromise" seems weighted against Paul, however.

22. This argument, and those that follow, cannot be dismissed simply by noting their similarity to Baur's *Tendenzkritik* which pointed to similar conflicts in the primitive church. Precisely this kind of evidence gave that thesis its persuasive power for so long. The differences between my conclusions and those of Baur are clear to any who are familiar with the latter's work.

23. Some scholars have suggested that the "superlative apostle" Paul is combating in 2 Corinthians 10—13 may have been Peter, even suggesting that Paul's "thorn in the flesh" which is a "messenger from Satan" (cf. Matt. 16:23!) may in fact have been the Prince of the apostles himself. A good discussion of this rather speculative view and the evidence cited for it can be found in Smith, *Petrine Controversies in Early Christianity*, 194–95.

24. Evidence for this comes from Tertullian, *de Praescriptione Haereticorum* 23, and is mentioned as well in his treatise *Against Marcion* 4.3 and 5.3, where he cites the right hand of fellowship (Gal. 2:9) as a sign of the acceptability of Peter (!). Irenaeus also cited Gal. 2:8 for the same purpose in *Against Heresies* 3.13.1. I owe these references to Smith, *Petrine Controversies*, 103–4, 209.

25. Ibid., 103.

26. For a good discussion of various positions in this dispute, see ibid., 157–59; cf. also 198.

27. Given the nature of the Pseudo-Clementine documents, any source derived from them would be both Jewish-Christian and anti-Pauline. The ele-

ments of a "Kerygma Petrou" derived on the other hand from Clement of Alexandria show neither tendency; it was from that source that von Dob-schütz made his reconstruction (with one or two references to comparable passages in Origen's commentary on the Gospel of John). See von Dobschütz, *Das Kerygma Petri Kritisch Untersucht*, esp. "Die Herstellung des Textes," 18–26.

28. For a more detailed discussion of these points, see again Smith, *Petrine Controversies*, 59–60.

29. Molland has argued that in six places that reflect the catechetical instruction carried on by the Christian group that produced this literature, five of them apparently drawn from the Kerygmata Petrou, reference to the Apostolic Decree can be detected ("La circoncision, le baptême et l'authorité du décret apostolique (Actes XV, 28 sq.) dans le milieux judéo-chrétiens des Pseudo-Clémentines," *ST* 9 (1955): pass., summarized on 39).

30. The Greek words are taken from the formulation of the Apostolic Decree that, Luke reports, was found in the letter sent out from the Jerusalem Council (Acts 15:20). I cite them to indicate to which of the four elements of that decree reference is being made.

31. Chap. 34. Quotation from *Writings of Saint Justin Martyr*, 200.

32. The quotation is from *Tertullian, Apologetical Works; Minucius Felix, Octavius*, 33. In 9.14, Tertullian mentions that one of the tests to see if an accused person was in fact a Christian was to offer them blood-filled sausages, indicating that the aversion to eating blood was widespread among Christians, and recognized by the Roman authorities.

33. "We have nothing to do with the Jews on any of these points: the taboo on certain kinds of food (sic!), the observance of certain holy days, the bodily 'seal' . . . " (ibid., 61). In this passage the much misunderstood phrase *religio licita* ("sub umbraculo insignissimae religionis, certe licitae," *Apology* 21.1), here referring to Judaism, occurs for the first time in Latin literature.

34. The claim by Dunn, typical of what I have earlier termed the "optimistic" interpretation of the evidence, that "though Paul lost the debate at Antioch his subsequent success as missionary to the Gentiles ensured the victory of his views in the longer term" ("Incident at Antioch," 40) is virtually the polar opposite of what did in fact happen. Paul's loss at Antioch colored not only his career as missionary, but the understanding of the faith for decades, if not centuries, to come.

35. There are many, most recently Oscar Cullmann (*Einheit durch Vielfalt*), who have recognized that unity in the contemporary church not only can but must embrace diversity. But Cullmann grounds that diversity in the variety of spiritual gifts of which Paul speaks in 1 Corinthians 12 rather than on the historical disunity within the early church. All who speak of the "recovery" of church unity fail in my view to understand the true situation of the early church.

CHAPTER 8
HISTORICAL REPORTING AND THE PURPOSE OF ACTS

1. The language and mode of argument are taken from Boice, "The Reliability of the Writings of Luke and Paul," *Christianity Today* 12 (1967): 8–10. While this is a more popular treatment, scholarly articles on the same topic from this perspective would proceed in the same way, although they would of course be equipped with more of the accoutrements of learned debate.

2. Ibid., 8.

3. These examples were drawn from Fitzmyer, *The Gospel According to Luke (I–IX)*, 15. Further evidence on why these passages are problems can be gleaned from consulting the articles on key words in such works as *Harper's Bible Dictionary* (ed. P. J. Achtemeier [San Francisco: Harper & Row, 1985]), or at the appropriate passages in commentaries such as Fitzmyer's two-volume work on Luke, or Haenchen's treatment of Acts.

4. I do not wish here to become involved in the question of the possibility of historical "objectivity" or even the theoretical problem of the possibility or value of "historical truth." The Hellenistic world did not share our modern prejudice that to prove a thing true it must be proved to be historical. For them, a thing was proved true if it could be shown to be traditional. But aside from that, the question I am raising concerns the popular understanding of history—namely, does the narrative reflect what happened, or did the author color his or her account to the extent that the order of events and their description in the narrative no longer reflect the order and content of what occurred? That is what is involved in the popular question of the "reliability" or "accuracy" of Acts, as a brief look at the literature where that question is raised will show; see also nn. 1 and 2 of the present chapter.

5. For an excellent discussion of the kinds of literary genres to which Acts has been compared, and the purpose of Acts within its own historical period, see Pervo, "Luke-Acts: The Eye of the Storm" in *Profit with Delight*.

6. I am indebted, in the discussion of this aspect of Luke, to Fitzmyer, *Gospel According to Luke*, 10, 16.

7. One should not be too quick to dismiss the concern for historical accuracy among ancient historians. Quintilian, for example, in defining three forms of narrative (fictitious, realistic, and historical), says that historical narrative "is an exposition of actual fact" (*Institutio Oratio*) 2.4.2, LCL 1, 225. Again Lucian of Samosata, a second-century author and satirist, claims that the peculiar character of history is that it must be true, and the historian must tell things as they happened ("How to Write History," pars. 39–40; the text can be found in *Lucian*, trans. K. Kilburn, LCL, 1968, 6:55). Lucian is emphasizing that a good historian does not distort or suppress facts to curry favor or flatter those in power, but the more general notion that a historian must present a true account of events nevertheless does come through (my attention

was called to the passages in Lucian by Fitzmyer, *Gospel According to Luke,* 16).

8. The RSV "undertaken to compile a narrative" is too bland for Luke's language; cf. Fitzmyer, who in his notes ventures the more colorful and more accurate "have set their hand to arrange in proper order an account" (*Gospel According to Luke,* 291–92) rather than his blander "have undertaken to compile an orderly account" (ibid., 287), which is nevertheless superior to the RSV.

9. The *anōthen* (here "from the beginning") in this verse refers, in light of v. 2, not to Luke's having paid careful attention to the *events* from the beginning —he has already said in v. 2 that he is not one of those eyewitnesses— but to his paying close attention to all of those *traditions,* including those that tell about the very beginnings of the Jesus movement that he is narrating.

10. See n. 4 of the present chapter.

11. Tacitus reserves to himself the right, in his *Histories,* of inserting in his work "whenever the *theme* or situation demands" examples "drawn from our earlier history" (*Histories* 3.51; emphasis mine). Similarly, Suetonius regularly draws anecdotes from other periods to illustrate a point he is making, indicating that his purpose in his "Lives of the Caesars" is not strict chronological order. In his life of *The Deified Julius,* for example, he interrupts his narrative of the things Caesar did on his return to Rome after his victories in the civil wars, and his ensuing death, to tell (beginning with chap. 45) a series of anecdotes about Caesar's personal appearance, motives for his actions both military and civil, and his sexual and literary exploits, among other things, with no regard for the chronological order of the anecdotes he relates, or for their relevance to the point he had reached in the narrative.

12. Talbert, *What Is a Gospel?,* 92–113.

13. Funk points out that the narrative unfolds in panels, moving "from Jerusalem through Judea and Samaria, Antioch, Asia, Greece to Rome" ("The Enigma of the Famine Visit," *JBL* 75 (1956): 134); he also points out that the second half of the book shows how Luke deals with materials on a geographical basis: Galatia, Macedonia, Achaia, Ephesus, and Rome. I owe to Funk the observation that once activity in an area is concluded, little more is said about it (ibid., 134).

14. Ibid., 134. His study on the famine visit of Acts 11:27–30 also contains an excellent review on this problem; typical of his careful scholarship is the wealth of other information on Lukan order he includes (esp. 133–36), and upon which I have drawn.

15. So Fitzmyer, *Gospel According to Luke,* 300.

16. This reflects Fitzmyer's conclusion that the Gospel (and by implication, I believe, Acts) reflects the author's "theological program" (a phrase borrowed from G. Klein), which is set out in the prologue and is "guided by promise and fulfillment" (ibid., 290).

NOTES

CHAPTER 9
REFLECTIONS ON SOME UNTRADITIONAL CONCLUSIONS

1. That is of course not an exclusively modern insight; see, e.g., the Augsburg Confession, chap. 20: "Faith is not merely a knowledge of historical events. . . . [It] mean[s the] assurance that God is gracious to us, and not merely such a knowledge of historical events as the devil also possesses."

2. Barrett has aptly noted that "Canon . . . does not mean an infallible account of historical events" ("Apostles in Council and in Conflict," *Aus BR* 31 [1983]: 26). Nor, as Fitzmyer has pointed out, does inspiration of the Bible "make history out of what was not such or intended to be such" (*The Gospel According to Luke (I–IX)*, 17–18).

3. Knox attempted to develop an account of Paul's career based solely on Paul's letters, but he did not compare the problem to that faced by the author of Acts (*Chapters in a Life of Paul*, chap. 2).

4. Plutarch thought those in peril, and the unfortunate, could boast and extol themselves with better grace than the fortunate ("On Inoffensive Self-Praise 541 A," in *Plutarch's Moralia*, LCL, 1959, 7:125). Quintilian noted that the most perverted and ostentatious kind of boasting took the form of self-derision, in which one claimed to be what one was not: e.g., the powerful claim they are weak (*Institutio Oratorio* 11.1.21, LCL, 1936, 4:167.) That Paul was aware of the devices by which self-praise might be ameliorated will be clear to anyone who compares 2 Corinthians 11–13 with Plutarch's "On Inoffensive Self-Praise." Unless, therefore, Paul was telling the truth about himself, he was open to a charge of perverse self-praise.

5. On the "messenger of Satan" as Peter, see chap. 7, n. 23.

6. On this "eschatological reservation" (Käsemann), see Rom. 6:5, 8, and 1 Cor. 15:49, among other similar passages. Its applicability to Paul's life as an apostle is clear in such a passage as Phil. 3:10–12.

7. I find little reason to think a visible sign of God's approval represented by the achievement of theological victories would not have fallen under the same condemnation of "confidence in the flesh" under which Paul placed his Jewish birthright, with its visible signs of God's acceptance in circumcision and the law; see the whole discussion in Phil. 3:3–13.

APPENDIX 1
THE APOSTOLIC DECREE

1. Tissot, noting the difference, argues that the former is the original form ("Les Prescriptions des Presbytres (Actes, XV, 41, D)" *RB* 77 [1970]: 342).

2. Manns argues that this substitution did not alter the original intention ("Remarques sur Acts 15,20.29," *Antonianum* 53 [1978]: 443–51.

3. Manek argues that *pniktou* was a gloss, albeit a very old one ("Das Aposteldekret im Kontext," *CV* 15 [1972]: 152).

4. Molland notes the two different possibilities ("La circoncision, le baptême et l'authorité du décret apostolique (Actes XV, 28 sq.) dans le milieux judéo-chrétiens des Pseudo-Clementines," *ST* 9 [1955]: 34); Manek argues that it must refer to a prohibition against murder ("Aposteldekret," 151).

5. Zuntz, "Analysis of . . . Apostolic Council," 225.

6. Boman, "Das Textkritische Problem des sogennanten Aposteldekrets," *NovT* 7 (1964): 32; and Tissot, "Prescriptions," pass.

7. Menoud, "The Western Text and the Theology of Acts," Bulletin of the *Studiorum, Novi Testamenti Societas* 2 (1951): 19–21. For further discussion, see Kümmel, "Die Älteste Form des Aposteldekrets."

8. Catchpole, "Paul, James and the Apostolic Decree," *NTS* 23 (1977): 429; and Zuntz, "Analysis of . . . Apostolic Council," 228.

9. Malina, "Does *Porneia* Mean Fornication?" *NovT* 14 (1972): 10–17.

10. Kümmel, "Die Älteste Form," 95.

11. Molland ("La circoncision," 38) finds this confirmed in the Pseudo-Clementines (*Recognition* 4.36; 6.10; *Homily* 8.23).

12. Simon, "The Apostolic Decree and its Setting in the Ancient Church," *BJRL* 52 (1970): 446–51.

13. Baur, *Paul, Apostle of Jesus Christ*, 142; and Haenchen, *Die Apostelgeschichte*, 459.

14. Peter Klein, "Zum Verständnis von Gal. 2:1 . . . ," *ZNW* 60 (1979): 251.

15. Malina, "Does *Porneia* Mean Fornication?" 13.

16. Moore, *Judaism*, 1: 274–75.

17. E.g., Molland, "La circoncision," 37–38.

18. E.g., Catchpole, "Paul, James and the Apostolic Decree," 430; Conzelmann, *Die Apostelgeschichte*, 85; Haenchen, *Die Apostelgeschichte*, 468–69; Perrot, "L'Assemblée de Jérusalem," *RSR* 69 (1981): 196; Simon, "The Apostolic Decree," 438–40; Zuntz, "Analysis of . . . Apostolic Council," 26.

19. Baur, *Paul, Apostle of Jesus Christ*, 141; Boman, "Textkritische Problem," 31–32; Manns, "Remarques," 448–49.

20. Boman, "Textkritische Problem," 31–32.

21. Manek, "Das Aposteldekret im Kontext," 153.

APPENDIX 2
LUKE AND THE SHAPING OF ACTS 15

1. The point here is that Luke did not invent his assumptions or "tendencies" out of whole cloth, nor did they represent some sort of unreasonable prejudices, unjustifiable by any standard. Any historian must make assumptions about the importance, as well as the order and arrangement, of the evi-

NOTES

dence at hand, and those assumptions in turn will have been drawn from the evidence itself. I want to urge that this was also the case with the author of Acts. Luke's "tendencies" represent assumptions he drew from his evidence, and then applied in cases where the evidence was not clear.

2. See, for example, Haenchen, *Die Apostelgeschichte*, 459; Barrett, "Apostles in Council and in Conflict," *Aus BR* 31 (1983): 21.

3. Braun suggested this particular solution in "James' Use of Amos at the Jerusalem Council: Steps toward a Possible Solution of the Textual and Theological Problems," (*JEvTS* 20 (1977): 113–21.

4. E.g., Barrett: the council was a creation of Luke although the decree itself rests on traditional material ("Apostles in Council and in Conflict," 23–24); Haenchen: Luke composed the account of the council as a climax in his narrative (*Die Apostelgeschichte*, 460); Catchpole: Lukan theology is sufficient to explain the association of decree with conference ("Paul, James and the Apostolic Decree," *NTS* 23 [1977]: 428); Borse: Luke added the decree when he enlarged his own shorter first edition ("Kompositionsgeschichtliche Beobachtungen zum Apostelkonzil," 195 and pass.). Mussner, on the other hand, finds no reason to doubt the historical association of the decree with the Jerusalem council ("Die Bedeutung des Apostelkonzils für die Kirche," 37). Others have argued that both are historical, but the decree originated later than the council (Pesche, "Das Jerusalemer Abkommen und die Lösung des Antiochenischen Konflikts," 105; Tissot, "Les Prescriptions des Presbytres (Actes, XV 41, D)," *RB* 77 (1970): 21.

5. Haenchen finds a progression in respect to Luke's references to elders: 11:30, elders introduced; 15:1, elders named with apostles; 21:18, elders named as sole authorities (*Das Apostelgeschichte*, 462). Pesch attributes their first mention in 11:30 to Lukan redactional activity, derived from their mention in 15:2 ("Das Jerusalemer Abkommen," 111); Mussner, on the other hand, suggests that the elders assumed prominence when James took over the leadership in Jerusalem ("Die Bedeutung," 39).

6. Gaechter, "Geschichtliches zum Apostelkonzil," *ZKT* 85 (1963): 345.

7. So J. N. Sanders, "Peter and Paul in Acts," *NTS* 2 (1955): 142.

8. So ibid., 135; Fischer (others from Antioch, but not Paul, were present), "Das Sogennante Apostelkonzil," 15, a position for which I also would argue.

9. E.g., Tissot (Luke knew "un document conciliaire"), "Les Prescriptions," 340–41; Bultmann, "Zur Frage nach den Quellen der Apostelgeschichte," 417; Doemer, *Das Heil Gottes; Studien zur Theologie des Lukanischen Doppelwerkes*, 180. Pesch suggests that Acts 11 and 15 represent Luke's attempt to make two meetings from an original account of only one ("Das Jerusalemer Abkommen," 114, 116–18).

10. Dillon and Fitzmyer point to Acts 15 as a passage that "argues for the theory of sources," "Acts of the Apostles," 194. For summaries of attempts to isolate various sources underlying Acts, see Marshall, "Recent Study of the

115

Acts of the Apostles," *Exp Tim* 80 (1968–69): 292–96; Manns, "Remarques sur Actes 15,20.29," *Antonianum* 53 (1978): 443–51; Weiser, "Das 'Apostelkonzil' (Apg 15,1–35)," *BZ*, NF 28 (1984): par. 3.1 (Weiser himself finds it possible to differentiate in detail between sources and editorial composition). Martin has found certain syntactical evidence that he feels points specifically to Aramaic sources underlying this narrative in Acts ("Syntactical Evidence of Aramaic Sources in Acts I–XV," *NTS* 11 [1964]: 38–59).

11. The position is well stated in Strecker, "Die sogennante zweite Jerusalemsreise des Paulus," *ZNW* 53 (1962): 69–70.

12. Dibelius, "The Apostolic Council," 93–101, esp. 98, had already argued that Acts 15 presumes its literary context, particularly those accounts contained in chaps. 10—11; cf. also Conzelmann, *Die Apostelgeschichte*, 87; Haenchen, *Die Apostelgeschichte*, 496; J. N. Sanders, "Peter and Paul in Acts," 138; Strecker, "Die sogennante zweite Jerusalemsreise des Paulus," 70–71; Zuntz, "Analysis . . . of Apostolic Council," pass., among many others. For arguments to the contrary, namely, that Luke faithfully recorded actual historical events, see Gaechter, "Geschichtliches zum Apostelkonzil," pass.; Boice, "The Reliability of the Writings of Luke and Paul," *Christianity Today* 12 (1967): 8–10.

13. This is not to say that Luke composed his narrative with no knowledge of any traditions whatsoever. Few if any scholars would assert that. It is rather a matter of the nature of those sources, whether written or oral, and the extent of their reliability. Some make as strong a case for the historical reliability of such oral traditions as Luke may have had (e.g., Gasque, "Did Luke Have Access to Traditions about the Apostles and the Early Church?" *JEvTS* 17 [1974]: 45–48) as others do for written sources.

APPENDIX 3
PAUL AND THE APOSTOLIC DECREE

1. So Dillon and Fitzmyer, "Acts of the Apostles," 196.

2. Mussner, "Die Bedeutung des Apostelkonzils für die Kirche," 38.

3. Conzelmann, *Die Apostelgeschichte*, 85; Fahy, "The Council of Jerusalem," *ITQ* 30 (1963): 248; Oepke, *Der Brief Paulus an die Galater*, 53.

4. E.g., Simon, "The Apostolic Decree and its Setting in the Ancient Church," *BJRL* 52 (1970): 452–54; Perrot, "L'Assemblée de Jerusalem," *RSR* 69 (1981): 207.

5. Hurd, *The Origin of 1 Corinthians*, 254–59.

6. E.g., Schlier, *Der Brief an die Galater*, 77.

7. Boman, "Das Textkritische Problem des sogennanten Aposteldekrets," *NT* 7 (1964): 34.

8. Strobel, "Das Aposteldekret in Galatien . . . ," *NTS* 20 (1974): 183.

9. In this I agree with Parker, "Once More, Acts and Galatians," *JBL* 86 (1967): 176.

10. Hoerber, "Galatians 2:1–10 and the Acts of the Apostles," *CTM* 31 (1960): 491 n. 19.

11. E.g., Murphy-O'Connor "Pauline Missions Before the Jerusalem Conference," *RB* 89 (1982): 71–91.

BIBLIOGRAPHY

PRIMARY SOURCES

Apostolic Fathers. Trans. K. Lake. 2 vols. LCL. 1952.

Eusebius. *The Ecclesiastical History.* Trans. K. Lake. 2 vols. LCL. 1965.

Justin Martyr. *Writings of Saint Justin Martyr.* Trans. T. B. Falls. The Fathers of the Church, a New Translation. New York: Christian Heritage, 1948.

Pseudo-Clementine Literature. *Recognitions of Clement; The Clementine Homilies.* Trans. T. Smith. The Ante-Nicene Fathers, vol. 8. New York: Charles Scribner's Sons, 1899.

Quintilian. *The Institutio Oratio of Quintilian.* Trans. E. Butler. 4 vols. LCL. New York: G. P. Putnam's Sons, 1933.

Suetonius. *The Lives of the Caesars.* Trans. J. C. Rolfe. 2 vols. LCL. 1970.

Tacitus. *The Histories.* Trans. C. H. Moore. 2 vols. LCL. New York: G. P. Putnam's Sons, 1931.

Tertullian. *Tertullian, Apologetical Works; Minucius Felix, Octavius.* Trans. E. K. Daly. The Fathers of the Church, a New Translation, 10. New York: Christian Heritage, 1950.

SECONDARY SOURCES

Aus, Roger D. "Three Pillars and Three Patriarchs: A Proposal Concerning Gal. 2:9." *ZNW* 70 (1979): 252–61.

Barrett, C. K. "Apostles in Council and in Conflict." *Aus BR* 31 (1983): 14–32.

Bauer, Walter. *Orthodoxy and Heresy in Earliest Christianity.* Trans. Philadelphia Seminar on Christian Origins. Ed. R. A. Kraft and G. Krodel. Philadelphia: Fortress Press, 1971.

Baur, Ferdinand Christian. *Paul, Apostle of Jesus Christ.* Trans. E. Zeller, Rev. A. Menzies. Edinburgh: Williams & Norgate, 1876.

Beck, Samuel Harris, III. "The Role of the Jerusalem Conference in the Acts of the Apostles." Ph.D. diss., Southern Baptist Theological Seminary, Louisville, Kentucky, 1973.

Betz, Hans Dieter. *Galatians.* (Hermeneia). Philadelphia: Fortress Press, 1979.

Boice, James Montgomery. "The Reliability of the Writings of Luke and Paul." *Christianity Today* 12 (1967): 8–10.

Boman, Thorlief. "Das Textkritische Problem des sogennanten Aposteldekrets." *Nov T* 7 (1964): 26–36.

Bornkamm, Günther. *Paul.* Trans. D. M. G. Stalker. New York: Harper & Row, 1971.

Borse, Udo. "Kompositionsgeschichtliche Beobachtungen zum Apostelkonzil." In *Begegnung mit dem Wort: Festschrift für Heinrich Zimmermann,* ed. J. Zmijewski, E. Nellessen, 195–212. Bonn: Peter Hanstein Verlag, 1980.

Braun, Michael A. "James' Use of Amos at the Jerusalem Council: Steps toward a Possible Solution of the Textual and Theological Problems." *JEvTS* 20 (1977): 113–21.

Bronson, David E. "Paul, Galatians, and Jerusalem." *JAAR* 35 (1967): 119–28.

Brown, Raymond E. *The Church the Apostles Left Behind.* New York: Paulist Press, 1984.

———. *Community of the Beloved Disciple.* New York: Paulist Press, 1979.

———. *The Epistles of John.* AB 30. New York: Doubleday & Co., 1982.

Brox, Norbert. *Der Erste Petrusbrief.* EKK. Zurich: Benziger Verlag, 1979.

Bruce, F. F. "Further Thoughts on Paul's Autobiography." In *Jesus und Paulus: Festschrift für Werner Georg Kümmel,* ed. E. E. Ellis and E. Graesser, 21–29. Göttingen: Vandenhoeck & Ruprecht, 1975.

Bultmann, Rudolf. "Zur Frage nach den Quellen der Apostelgeschichte." In *Exegetica, Aufsätze zur Erforschung des NT,* ed. E. Dinkler, 412–23. Tubingen: J. C. B. Mohr, 1967.

Burchard, Christoph. "Paulus in der Apostelgeschichte." *TLZ* 100 (1975): 882–96.

Cambier, J. "Le Voyage de S. Paul à Jérusalem en Act. ix.26ss. et la Schéma Missionnaire Théologique de s. Luc." *NTS* 8 (1962): 249–57.

Catchpole, R. "Paul, James and the Apostolic Decree." *NTS* 23 (1977): 428–44.

Conzelmann, Hans. *Die Apostelgeschichte.* HNT. Tübingen: J. C. B. Mohr (Paul Siebeck), 1963 (Eng. trans: *Acts.* Hermeneia. Philadelphia: Fortress Press, 1987).

Cullmann, Oscar. *Einheit durch Vielfalt.* Tübingen: J. C. B. Mohr (Paul Siebeck), 1986 (Eng. trans: *Unity through Diversity.* Philadelphia: Fortress Press, 1987).

Dibelius, Martin. "The Apostolic Council." In *Studies in the Acts of the Apostles,* 93–101. London: SCM Press, 1956.

Dillon, R. A. and J. A. Fitzmyer. "Acts of the Apostles." In *JBC,* 165–214.

Dobschütz, Ernst von. *Das Kerygma Petri Kritisch Untersucht.* Ed. O. von Geb-

119

hardt and A. von Harnack. Texte und Untersuchungen 11. Leipzig: J. C. Hinrichs'sche Buchhandlung, 1894.

Doemer, Michael. *Das Heil Gottes; Studien zur Theologie des Lukanischen Doppelwerkes.* Bonn: Peter Hanstein Verlag, 1980.

Duncan, George S. *The Epistle of Paul to the Galatians.* London: Hodder & Stoughton, 1934.

Dunn, James D. G. "The Incident at Antioch." *JSNT* 18 (1983): 3–57.

———. "The Relationship between Paul and Jerusalem according to Galatians 1 and 2." *NTS* 28 (1982): 461–78.

———. *Unity and Diversity in the New Testament.* Philadelphia: Westminster Press, 1977.

Eckert, Jost. "Paulus und die Jerusalemer Authoritäten nach dem Galaterbrief und der Apostelgeschichte." In *Schriftauslegung,* ed. J. Ernst, 281–311. Munich: Ferdinand Schoeningh, 1972.

Elliott, J. K. "Jerusalem in Acts and the Gospels." *NTS* 23 (1977): 462–69.

———. "Κηφᾶς: Σίμων Πέτρος: ὁ Πέτρος: An Examination of New Testament Usage." *Nov T* 14 (1972): 241–56.

Enslin, Morton S. "Emphases and Silences." *HTR* 73 (1980): 219–25.

———. "Once Again, Luke and Paul." *ZNW* 61 (1970): 253–71.

Fahy, T. "The Council of Jerusalem." *ITQ* 30 (1963): 233–61.

Filson, Floyd V. "Live Issues in the Acts." In *Biblical Research,* 9:26–37. Chicago: Chicago Society of Biblical Research, 1964.

Fischer, Joseph A. "Das Sogennante Apostelkonzil." In *Konzil und Papst: Festgabe für Hermann Tüchle,* ed. G. Schwaiger, 1–17. Munich: Ferdinand Schoeningh, 1975.

Fitzmyer, Joseph A. *The Gospel According to Luke (I–IX).* AB 28. Garden City, N.Y.: Doubleday & Co., 1981.

———. "The Letter to the Galatians." In *JBC,* 236–46.

Fung, Ronald Y. K. "A Note on Galatians 2:3–8." *JEvTS* 25 (1982): 49–52.

Funk, Robert W. "The Enigma of the Famine Visit." *JBL* 75 (1956): 130–36.

Gaechter, S. J. "Geschichtliches zum Apostelkonzil." *ZKT* 85 (1963): 339–54.

Gasque, Ward W. "Did Luke Have Access to Traditions about the Apostles and the Early Church?" *JEvTS* 17 (1974): 45–48.

Haenchen, Ernst. *Die Apostelgeschichte.* Series KEK. Göttingen: Vandenhoeck & Ruprecht, 1956.

Hainz, Joseph. "Gemeinschaft (*koinōnia*) zwischen Paulus und Jerusalem (Gal. 2:9f.)." In *Kontinuität und Einheit: Für Franz Mussner,* ed. P.-G. Müller and W. Stenger, 30–42. Freiburg: Herder, 1981.

Hall, David R. "St. Paul and Famine Relief: A Study in Galatians 2:10." *Exp Tim* 82 (1970–71): 309–11.

Hemer, Colin J. "Acts and Galatians Reconsidered." *Themelios* 2 (1977): 81–88.

BIBLIOGRAPHY

Hengel, Martin. *Acts and the History of Earliest Christianity.* Trans. J. Bowden. Philadelphia: Fortress Press, 1979.

Hoerber, Robert G. "Galatians 2:1–10 and the Acts of the Apostles." *CTM* 31 (1960): 482–91.

Hoerber, Robert O. "The Decree of Claudius in Acts 18:2." *CTM* 31 (1960): 690–94.

Holtz, Traugott. "Die Bedeutung des Apostelkonzils für Paulus." *NovT* 16 (1974): 110–48.

Hurd, John C., Jr. *The Origin of 1 Corinthians.* New York: Seabury Press, 1965.

Jeske, Richard L. "Luke and Paul on the Apostle Paul." *Cur TM* 4 (1977): 28–38.

Jewett, Robert. "The Agitators and the Galatians Congregation." *NTS* 17 (1970–71): 198–212.

Kesich, Veselin. "The Apostolic Council at Jerusalem." *St.VTQ* 6 (1962): 108–17.

Kilpatrick, G. D. "Peter, Jerusalem and Galatians 1:13—2:14." *NovT* 25 (1983): 318–26.

Klein, Günter. "Galater 2,6–9 und die Geschichte der Jerusalemer Urgemeinde." *ZTK* 57 (1960): 275–95.

Klein, Peter. "Zum Verständnis von Gal. 2:1 . . . " *ZNW* 60 (1979): 251 (sic).

Knox, John. *Chapters in a Life of Paul.* Nashville: Abingdon Press, 1950.

Koester, Helmut. *Introduction to the New Testament.* Trans. H. Koester. 2 vols. Philadelphia: Fortress Press, 1982.

Krodel, Gerhard. *Acts.* Proclamation Commentaries. Philadelphia: Fortress Press, 1981.

Kümmel, Werner Georg. "Die Älteste Form des Aposteldekrets." In *Spiritus et Veritas* (Festschrift Karl Kundsin), ed. Auseklis, Societas Theologorum Universitatis Latviensis. 1953.

Lyons, George. *Pauline Autobiography: Toward a New Understanding.* SBL DS 73. Atlanta: Scholars Press, 1985.

Malina, Bruce. "Does *Porneia* Mean Fornication?" *Nov T* 14 (1972): 10–17.

Manek, Mindrich. "Das Aposteldekret im Kontext." *CV* 15 (1972): 151–60.

Manns, Frederic. "Remarques sur Actes 15,20.29." *Antonianum* 53 (1978): 443–51.

Marshall, I. Howard. "Recent Study of the Acts of the Apostles." *Exp Tim* 80 (1968–69): 292–96.

Martin, R. A. "Syntactical Evidence of Aramaic Sources in Acts I–XV." *NTS* 11 (1964): 38–59.

Martyn, J. Louis. *History and Theology in the Fourth Gospel.* Rev. and enlarged ed. Nashville: Abingdon Press, 1979.

Menoud. Ph. H. "The Western Text and the Theology of Acts." Bulletin of *Studiorum Novi Testamenti Societas* 2 (1951): 19–32.

Molland, Einar. "La circoncision, le baptême et l'authorité du décret apostolique (Actes XV, 28 sq.) dans le milieux judéo-chrétiens des Pseudo-Clémentines." *ST* 9 (1955): 1–39.

Moore, George Foot. *Judaism*. 3 vols. Cambridge, Mass.: Harvard Univ. Press, 1946.

Murphy-O'Connor, J., O.B. "Pauline Missions Before the Jerusalem Conference." *RB* 89 (1982): 71–91.

Mussner, Franz. "Die Bedeutung des Apostelkonzils für die Kirche." In *Ekklesia* (Festschrift für M. Wehr), 35–46. Trier: Paulinus Verlag, 1962.

———. *Der Galaterbrief.* HTKNT. Freiburg: Herder, 1974.

Nesbitt, Charles F. "What Did Become of Peter?" *JBR* 27 (1959): 10–16.

Nickle, Keith F. *The Collection: A Study in Paul's Strategy*. London: SCM Press, 1966.

Nolland, J. L. "A Fresh Look at Acts 15:10." *NTS* 27 (1980): 105–15.

Oepke, Albrecht. *Der Brief Paulus an die Galater*. THKNT. Berlin: Evangelische Verlagsanstalt, 1957.

Panimolle, Salvatore Alberto. "L'Authorité de Pierre en *Ga* 1–2 et *AC* 15." In *Paul de Tarse, Apôtre du Notre Temps*, ed. L. de Lorenzi, 269–89. Rome: Abbaye de S. Paul, 1979.

Parker, Pierson. "Once More, Acts and Galatians." *JBL* 86 (1967): 175–82.

Perrot, C. "L'Assemblée de Jérusalem." *RSR* 69 (1981): 195–208.

Pervo, Richard I. *Profit with Delight: The Literary Genre of the Acts of the Apostles*. Philadelphia: Fortress Press, 1987.

Pesch, Rudolph. "Das Jerusalemer Abkommen und die Lösung des Antiochenischen Konflikts." In *Kontinuität und Einheit: Für Franz Mussner*, ed. P.-G. Müller and W. Stenger, 105–22. Freiburg: Herder, 1981.

Reicke, Bo. "Der geschichtliche Hintergrund des Apostelkonzils und der Antiochia-Episode, Gal. 2,1–14." In *Studia Paulina in honorem Johannes de Zwaan . . .* , ed. J. N. Sebenster and W. C. van Unnik, 173–87. Haarlem: Bohn, 1953.

Ross, J. M. "The Appointment of Presbyters in Acts xiv.23." *Exp Tim* 63 (1952): 288–89.

Sanders, J. N. "Peter and Paul in Acts." *NTS* 2 (1955): 133–43.

Sanders, Jack T. "Paul's 'Autobiographical' Statements in Galatians 1—2." *JBL* 85 (1966): 335–43.

Schlier, Heinrich. *Der Brief an die Galater*. Meyer K. Göttingen: Vandenhoeck & Ruprecht, 1949.

Scott, J. Julius, Jr. "Parties in the Church of Jerusalem as Seen in the Book of Acts." *JEvTS* 8 (1975): 217–27.

Simon, Marcel. "The Apostolic Decree and its Setting in the Ancient Church." *BJRL* 52 (1970): 437–60.

Smith, Terence V. *Petrine Controversies in Early Christianity*. WUNT 2. Reihe 15. Tübingen: J. C. B. Mohr (Paul Siebeck), 1985.

Smothers, Edgar R. "Chrysostom and Symeon (Acts xv, 14)." *HTR* 46 (1953): 203–15.

Stein, Robert H. "The Relationship of Galatians 2:1–10 and Acts 15:1–35: Two Neglected Arguments." *JEvTS* 17 (1974): 239–42.

Strecker, Georg. "Die sogennante zweite Jerusalemsreise des Paulus." *ZNW* 53 (1962): 67–77.

Strobel, August. "Das Aposteldekret als Folge des Antiochenischen Streites." In *Kontinuität und Einheit: Für Franz Mussner*, ed. P.-G. Müller and W. Stenger, 81–104. Freiburg: Herder, 1981.

———. "Das Aposteldekret in Galatien: zur Situation von Gal. I und II." *NTS* 20 (1974): 177–90.

Talbert, Charles H. "Again: Paul's Visits to Jerusalem." *Nov T* 9 (1967): 26–40.

———. *What Is a Gospel?* Philadelphia: Fortress Press, 1977.

Thompson, William G. *Matthew's Advice to a Divided Community; Mt. 17, 22—18,35.* An Bib 44. Rome: Biblical Institute Press, 1970.

Tissot, Yves. "Les Prescriptions des Presbytres (Actes, XV, 41, D)." *RB* 77 (1970): 321–46.

Toussaint, Stanley D. "The Chronological Problem of Galatians 2:1–10." *B Sac* 120 (1963): 334–40.

Wagley, Laurence A. and Eugene L. Lowry. "Homiletical Resources: Galatians, A Marvelous Book for Preachers." *Quarterly Review* 3, 1. (1983): 6–33.

Weeden, Theodore J. *Mark: Traditions in Conflict.* Philadelphia: Fortress Press, 1971.

Weiser, Alfons. "Das 'Apostelkonzil' (Apg 15,1–35)." *BZ*, NF 28 (1984): 145–67.

Wolfe, Charles E. "A New Path: How a Textual Variant Provides Additional Insight." *CM*, Jan. 1979, 19–21.

Zeitlin, Solomon. "Paul's Journey to Jerusalem." *JQR* 57 (1966–67): 171–78.

Zuntz, G. "An Analysis of the Report about the Apostolic Council." In *Opuscula Selecta*, 216–51. Cambridge: Manchester Univ. Press, 1972.

INDEXES

INDEX OF SCRIPTURE REFERENCES

124

INDEX OF ANCIENT AUTHORS

GENERAL INDEX

INDEX OF MODERN AUTHORS

n.2, 103–4 n.13, 104 n.18, 115
n.10, 116 n.1, 119
Dobschütz, Ernst von, 109–10 n.27,
119
Doemer, Michael, 115 n.9, 120
Duncan, George S., 101 n.1, 102 n.5,
108 n.13, 120
Dunn, James D. G., 95 nn.1, 3; 96
nn.7, 16; 97 n.18, 105 n.27, 106
n.31, 107 n.1, 108 nn.9, 12, 14, 15,
16; 109 nn.18, 19; 110 n.34, 120

Eckert, Jost, 93 n.8, 93–94 n.23, 105
n.22, 106 n.31, 108 n.8, 120
Elliott, J. K., 94 n.12, 96 n.9, 98
n.14, 100 n.4, 102 n.7, 120
Enslin, Morton Scott, 93 n.21, 98
n.3, 99 n.17, 108 n.13, 109 n.17,
120

Fahy, T., 96 n.15, 103–4 n.13, 104
n.19, 105 n.22, 116 n.3, 120
Filson, Floyd V., 107 n.3, 120
Fischer, Joseph A., 94 n.3, 96 n.9,
102 n.5, 115 n.8, 120
Fitzmyer, J. A., 93 n.16, 95 n.14, 96
n.16, 98 n.9, 100 n.2, 103–4 n.13,
104 n.18, 109 n.3, 110 n.6, 111–
12 n.7, 112 nn.8, 15, 16; 113 n.2
(chap. 9), 115 n.10, 116 n.1, 119,
120
Fung, Ronald Y. K., 96 n.10, 103
n.8, 120
Funk, Robert W., 95 n.16, 99 n.20,
101 n.1, 112 nn.13, 14; 120

Gaechter, S. J., 87, 93 n.19, 104–5
n.19, 116 n.12, 120
Gasque, Ward W., 116 n.13, 120

Haenchen, E., 14, 98 n.8, 99 n.13,
100 nn.2, 3; 103 n.9, 110 n.3, 114
nn.13, 18; 115 nn.2, 5; 116 n.12,
120
Hainz, Joseph, 99 n.16, 120
Hall, David R., 97 n.14, 102 n.5, 103
n.11, 120
Hemer, Colin J., 102 nn.4, 5; 120

Hengel, Martin, 18, 95 n.16, 96
nn.8, 13; 98 n.12, 99 n.15, 100
n.7, 105 n.28, 121
Hoerber, Robert G., 90, 96 n.15, 102
n.4, 107 n.1, 121
Hoerber, Robert O., 121
Holtz, Traugott, 95 n.6, 99 nn.15,
16; 107 n.1, 108 n.8, 121
Hurd, John C., Jr., 89, 94 nn.6, 9,
12; 96–97 n.17, 98 nn.10, 12;
103–4 n.13, 121

Jeske, Richard L., 93 n.8, 121
Jewett, Robert, 99 n.16, 100 n.8, 106
n.30, 107 n.1, 121

Kesich, Veselin, 93 n.22, 102 n.4,
105 n.20, 106 n.30, 107 n.1, 121
Kilpatrick, G. D., 96 n.9, 121
Klein, Günter, 114 n.14, 121
Knox, John, 7, 8, 45, 93 nn.7, 17; 99
n.18, 100 n.2, 101 n.11, 103 n.11,
107 n.5, 113 n.3, 121
Koester, Helmut, 108 n.9, 121
Krodel, Gerhard, 98 n.13, 105 n.24,
107 n.1, 121
Kümmel, Werner Georg, 114 nn.7,
10; 121

Lyons, George, 97 n.1, 100 n.8, 121

Malina, Bruce, 114, nn.9, 15; 121
Manek, Mindrich, 85, 107 n.34, 109
n.21, 114 nn.3, 4; 121
Manns, Frederic, 113 n.2 (Appendix
1), 114 n.19, 115–16 n.10, 121
Marshall, I. Howard, 97 n.2, 115
n.10, 121
Martin, R. A., 115–16 n.10, 121
Martyn, J. Louis, 92 n.5, 121
Menoud, Ph. H., 114 n.7, 121
Molland, Einar, 110 n.29, 114 nn.4,
11, 17; 122
Moore, George Foot, 114 n.16, 122
Murphy-O'Connor, J., 92 n.3, 107
n.1, 108–9 n.16, 117 n.11, 122
Mussner, Franz, 92 n.2 (chap. 1), 93
nn.9, 23; 98 n.12, 100 n.7, 104–5